Redefine Your Purpose, Restart The Nation

Chukwunwike Enekwechi

Restartnaija

ISBN: 9798469523396

DEDICATION

This book is dedicated to all devoted
educationists and sincere disciplinarians all
over the world. Second, it is dedicated to all of
Schoenstatt family and the family of Sir
Sylvanus Enekwechi, both of whose
disciplined formation shaped my life. Third, it
is dedicated to all associates of Restartnaija,
Appolus Chu Foundation and those who
believe in the progress of humanity.

CONTENTS

Chapter 1

WHY IS MAN ON EARTH?

*"Without knowing its destination,
The best ship wanders purposelessly on the sea."*
– Arnold Schwarzenegger

A trip to the Amazon Rainforest gives you a thrilling effect about the power and beauty of nature. It is a reserved nature-corner with uninterrupted wildlife that retains the texture and reference to human origin. The crudeness of the wild plants, animals, insects, stones and waterbodies in their natural state and unpolluted habitats draw human mind to its origin. When you visit this calm, natural and beautiful place or other natural reserves, you experience the type of peace that is lacking in the bustling and hustling megacities and urban areas. In such places, you feel alive, reconnect to your natural source and feel more responsive to nature. You suddenly feel your mind crack open, lose inhibitions, sing, laugh, view animals moving in groups and acting according to nature; you listen to birds, walk on bare ground, swim in natural streams, pluck and eat fresh fruits without genetic modification and artificial boosts. In such environments, humans recharge their minds from Mother Nature and get inspiration for social and scientific creativity from interacting directly with the uncontaminated form of nature.

A comparison between the crudeness in the amazon rainforest and the material advancement in the cities shows that humans have made great progress in science and technology. They have been great agents of progress in the world. In two centuries, the leap from the industrial revolution eclipsed the scientific efforts and industrial progress of the preceding million years of human existence. The genius behind the progress in agriculture, industry, communication, transportation, sports, entertainment, security, housing, research, education, medical investigations, treatments, trade and social organization continues to surprise us as humans.

- With the help of technology, the time, resources and labour required in cultivating food have reduced drastically. Now, the same amount of energy previously required for an acre of land in two days can be used to cultivate twenty acres of land even in a shorter time.
- Several people in far distant locations can have a formal meeting, seeing one another without being physically present in the same country, continent or planet.
- Through science and technology, many diseases that had eluded detection and treatment are now detected and treated with efficient machines, technique and pharmaceutical remedies.
- Modern cars, trains, phones, computers, houses and machines easily perform excellent tasks that were formerly considered difficult or outright impossible.

<u>Man as the central force of nature</u>

The continuous manifestation of creativity in social organization, scientific productivity and ecological control shows man's central position in nature. Man is at the heart of nature[1], for every question about sky, moon, stars, air, water, atoms, cells, even God become relevant only with reference to man's being.[2] Every object in nature has some important function to perform for the sustenance of other objects in nature. Grass becomes food for goat, goat becomes food for lion, lion later dies and become manure for grass, and other goats eat the grass, and so on. Like in this cycle, there are still many uses for different plants, animals, insects, waterbodies, gases, rocks and other elements. Humans have not yet discovered the proper use for many of these objects and forces in nature. Yet, these objects and forces retain their capacities for contributing to the cycle of life. And any object's total disappearance from nature may later prove tragic to the cycle of life.

Thus, the central principles of nature are ***growth*** and ***harmony***.

---

[1] Protagoras, conferred from Joseph Omoregbe, *A simplified History of Western Philosophy,* (Joja press, Ikeja, Lagos, 1991), p.27.
[2] Battista Mondin, *Philosophical Anthropology,* (Rome: Urbaniana University press, 1985), p.1.

Growth is the process of increasing in size or capacity. Harmony is the state of sustainable coexistence between different objects such that one does not completely eliminate the other. These are the two principles that maintain a balance for co-existence between natural objects so that no one overgrows to totally eliminate others. Cold and heat, darkness and light, fire and water, sand and air, birth and death, strength and weakness are few of the tools that nature uses to harmonize growth in the universe. "For in nature, any specie that is overhunting and overexploiting, natural selection will sooner or later take the predator out."[3]

Being at the heart of nature, man continues the central role of enabling growth and harmony among natural entities to avoid anyone's extreme growth or total extinction.[4] So, humans enable endangered organisms and people to flourish and contribute their unique gifts to life. Also, humans tame, restrict or eliminate elements, organisms, people or social networks that overhunt to eliminate others from the cycle of life. Nature bestows reasoning, creativity and transcendence (responsibility) on humans to enable them study, evaluate, decide and act on objects and forces for growth and harmony. These three faculties are the basis for being a complete and authentic human being.

REASONING is the ability to think in a logical manner in order to evaluate and understand the present and past, or predict the future. It comes from studying the steadiness and relationship between causes and effects, or actions and results in nature.[5] For instance, we notice that if it rains (cause) the land will be wet (effect); if I slap you, you will feel pain; liquids flow downwards along the path of least resistance; metals change shape and form under intense heat. From such observations, humans draw patterns of beliefs for relating with the world. For without understanding and working with the forces and laws of nature, humans cannot make progress. Instead, they position themselves for nature's punishments in form of diseases, deaths, loss, accidents and natural disasters. So, by reasoning and researching on natural resources and forces, humans derive and promote essential beliefs for harmonious coexistence and scientific

---

[3] Mallence Bart-Williams, Change your channel, TED x Talks, 26th June 2015. m.youtube.com/watch?v=AfnruW7yERA

[4] Chukwunwike Enekwechi, "From Human to Patriot, more emotional than mechanical" in *Restartnaija,* 11th September, 2018. https://restartnaija.com/2018/09/11/human-patriot-emotional-mechanical/ retrieved 2nd November, 2018.

[5] Cf. Thomas Hobbes, *Leviathan,* edited by Michael Oakeshott (New York: Macmillan Publishing Company, 1962) p.37

productivity.[6] Since we are limited by time and space, we hold and use such beliefs in faith until future discoveries counter them.

CREATIVITY flows from human reasoning to use the objects and forces in the environment to satisfy their needs. For instance, knowing that liquids flow downwards along the path of least resistance and that metals change under heat, humans make tools from metals to create free paths for draining flood or make irrigation. So, creativity is discovering and using various methods and tools for managing human and natural resources to satisfy needs and solve problems. Through social creativity, humans organize societies to collaborate in using human and natural resources for solving their problems. The constant use of creativity to organize people, satisfy needs, produce useful items and solve problems is called productivity.

TRANSCENDENCE, here, is a level of universe-consciousness where we overcome or transcend personal biases in order to take responsibility for enabling and harmonizing growth in nature. It can be called morality to involve relating with people and environment for harmonious growth. Unlike other beings and animals, humans are responsible for their actions because we have the freewill to choose our actions.[7] In using productivity to satisfy needs and solve problems, we have the option to seek things that benefit only us even if it harms others, or to consider other people's wellbeing while seeking our wellbeing. Due to fear, greed and indifference, we tend to focus on satisfying only our personal desires, even at other peoples' expense. But in being transcendent, we think of other people's wellbeing while seeking our own.

Through reasoning, creativity and transcendence, humans build cities, fight diseases, hunger, life-threatening beasts and factors that threaten harmonized growth. Apart from controlling human and non-human threats to harmonious growth, they assist different elements in nature to develop and become useful to the cycle of life. Because of this universe responsibility or transcendence, humans now protect endangered species of plants and animals, and value human's harmonious growth, despite gender, race or faith.

These three qualities qualify humans as agents of growth and harmony. Yet, a person's reasoning and transcendence can only be seen in his productivity. If you claim to be responsible and reasonable, but you are not productive, or your productivity and actions are harming innocent people,

---

[6] Chukwunwike Enekwechi, "Is the truth always bitter?" in *Restartnaija,* 15th January, 2019. https://restartnaija.com/2019/01/15/the-truth-always-bitter/ retrieved 11th February, 2019.
[7] Paul Glenn, *A tour of the Summa of St. Thomas Aquinas,* (USA: Tan Books and Publishers Inc., 1978), p.101

you are either irresponsible or unreasonable. The effect of your productivity on the society is the main evidence of your reasoning and transcendence (responsibility). So, this book qualifies people as agents of growth and harmony based on their productivity and social responsibility. Without social responsibility, productivity becomes exploitation; and without productivity, social responsibility becomes ineffective noise.[8] This book also refers to all human actions that support social growth and harmony as positive social impact.

Happiness is man's ultimate goal

In performing human tasks, we are naturally inclined to seeking happiness. Aristotle insists that happiness is the meaning and purpose of life, the whole aim and end of human existence.[9] All our actions, efforts and relationships gear towards happiness, or are judged by their ability to provide happiness. We repeat activities from which we get happiness in order to retain the feeling. We acquire things, make friends, marry or work to be happy; and if these things stop making us happy, we withdraw from them. Due to varied influences and understandings of happiness, various people seek happiness through different contradictory sources. Thus, happiness can be classified into two, namely material and internal happiness.

- **Material Happiness** is the nice feeling you get from elements of food, shelter, sex and bragging rights or having and using goods and services just for yourself and/or your allies. It includes feelings from food, comfort, intimacy, friendship, entertainment, music, sports, skills, power, beauty, online/offline recognition, praise and other material and nonmaterial possessions. It is the joy from using or consuming things for personal pleasure. This is the feeling we share equally with animals for gathering, protecting or using different resources for your physical satisfaction. Animals enjoy food, power, territory, sex, comfort, affection, security, health, skills and other externally-derived feelings too. So this book uses material happiness interchangeably with ***animal happiness***.

Despite our physical nature, we have an active supernatural side that transcends the physical side. "All specifically human action is thick with spirituality: there is always something that evades the sphere of matter in

---

[8] Chukwunwike Enekwechi, "Let's make Nigeria great again… how great? We will get there… Where?" in Restartnaija 17th July, 2019. https://restartnaija.com/2019/07/17/lets-make-nigeria-great-again/ retrieved 30th July, 2019.
[9] Cf. Aristotle, Nicomachean ethics, p.1.

knowledge, will, speech, culture, technique, etc."[10] And man always finds himself unfulfilled, never satisfied on the throne of conquered material success,[11] thus, he seeks a supernatural happiness.[12][13] Our transcendent nature requires a higher level of happiness to fulfil the desire for meaningful life in being good, responsible and socially relevant, not just parasitic consumers and dustbins for other people's products. So, while securing resources for physical happiness, humans crave an internal purpose that **fulfils** their desire for meaningful life.

- **Internal happiness or fulfilment** is a surge of blissful satisfaction from discovering, developing and using your potentials, natural resources and products for harmonious growth in the world. While helping a needy, saving a drowning child, building communities for civilization or solving social problems, we feel internally happy as if our heart says: "yes, this is how I am supposed to be". This feeling rises in us because we have a transcendental dimension that makes us responsible for harmonizing growth. For humans are the only natural beings with rationality, creativity and responsibility for harmonious growth in the world. So, our internal happiness comes from responding to our yearning for improving the world. It does not just come from what we have, and cannot be given to us by other people. Instead, it comes as internal joy and approval for the rational and responsible things we do with what we have.

Early in life, we are filled with noble, bold and problem-solving intentions for a better world. We dream of ending poverty, hunger, diseases, crimes or problems in different parts of the world. But, we later grow in cultures of fear and greed that distract us from the initial sparks of heroism. Many people get damaged by abuses, wars, betrayals, heartbreaks, injustices or indoctrinations, such that they mainly relate with others from fear, greed or hatred. Despite the grip of fear, greed and hatred, we feel happy when we slightly express social responsibility. After acquiring a skill or qualification for enriching humanity, we feel glorious and internally cool. After breaking a positive record or getting solutions to some real problem, we feel the internal applause. This is the internal feeling of satisfaction we deeply crave to make life meaningful without depending on praise-singers and sycophants. *This book uses internal happiness interchangeably with true happiness, fulfilment or full measure of happiness.*

---

[10] Battista Mondin. Op. Cit. p.196.
[11] Battista Mondin, Op. Cit. p.196.
[12] Cf. Thomas Hobbes, *Leviathan,* edited by Michael Oakeshott (New York: Macmillan Publishing Company, 1962) p.51.
[13] Cf. Thomas Aquinas, *Summa Theologiae* Ia IIae question Part 2. Q1, a7-8.

<u>Foundation for material and true happiness
– resources and knowledge</u>

The noblest reward for human heart is internal happiness. Yet, to obtain either material or internal happiness, humans require products which come from scientific knowledge and natural resources. Therefore, *natural resources* and *knowledge* for making relevant items are the foundation for material and internal happiness. To satisfy their private needs or to help others, humans create wealth by applying scientific knowledge on natural resources like agricultural yields and mineral resources to make tools and useful products.[14] Having natural resources like gold without knowledge or knowledgeable people to develop, secure and use them will not bring useful products for yourself or for others. Also, having the knowledge or skill without having natural resources from which you produce useful items will not solve either your problem or other people's problems. So, without natural resources and knowledge for producing things to either help ourselves or help others, we may not get either material or internal happiness.

<u>Using resources and knowledge for material and true happiness
through security and pleasure</u>

Two basic ways of measuring people's happiness are security and pleasure. Security is the feeling of having sufficient resources to satisfy your needs and save you from attacks, disease, hunger, pain or loss. Pleasure is the nice feeling from using or relating with humans, resources, skills and different products. Both security and pleasure yield material happiness when sought just for ourselves; and bring internal happiness when sought for harmonized growth in the world.

Pleasure brings internal happiness by refreshing or preparing you to make social impact. But it brings destruction when it prevents you from developing yourself to harmonize growth. For instance, over-drinking or over-eating brings momentary pleasure, but is followed by illness, shame, misbehaviour, crime and violence, while modest intake helps you relax and recover your energy, zeal and inspiration for better productivity. The pleasure from applauding people's qualities, possessions and deeds can build their self-esteem and confidence to improve and contribute more. But the person who seeks all his applause from outside has his happiness in another's keeping.[15] Such persons become miserable when their good deeds

---

[14] Cf. Walter Rodney, *How Europe underdeveloped Africa, 2009 edition,* (Abuja: Panaf press, 2009) p.23.
[15] Dale Carnegie quoted in Alan Mason, *Business Bullseye: How to succeed in business,* (Canada: Broadview publishing, 2009), p.39.

or qualities are not seen or applauded by others.

When security is not aimed at internal happiness, it becomes vicious, leading to cruelty and greed. And when pleasure is not aimed at internal happiness through harmonizing growth, it becomes vicious, leading to gluttony, addictions and waste of material resources; or bitter rivalry, jealousy, boasting, lying, debt, theft and eye-service for applause. People can measure your material happiness from outside. But you know your level of internal happiness, or its emptiness, frustration and pain even while suppressing it with drugs, alcohol and external noises from music, over-activity, sycophants and material distractions. Despite the material distractions you employ to occupy your mind, the space for internal happiness remains empty in your life without social impact in harmonizing growth.

> *Trying to fill the space for internal happiness with animal happiness is like trying to quench your thirst for water with Vodka, rum, gin or other hot drinks. The thirst can only increase despite the amount of hot drinks you ingest against it.* – Restartnaija

Challenges in man's search for happiness

Despite the material progress, efforts to get lasting happiness and reduce bitterness, depression, and limitations appear ineffective in many places. Incidents of depression and suicide even among the wealthy, emptiness of life, mass-shootings, wars, terrorism, nuclear threats, disasters and accidents challenge the absolute efficacy of material happiness in human destiny. As we struggle for different forms of happiness, billions of people suffer diseases, homelessness, poverty and emptiness of life. This challenges the motives through which we live and seek happiness.

Different motives with which humans seek happiness

The two varying motives with which we seek happiness can be distinguished as **"living to have"** and **"having to live"**. They help us answer the question about why we are on earth. **Living-to-have** means directing your life and abilities to having resources for personal pleasure: living to have money, wife, family, friends, job, comfort, titles, possessions, health, etc. On the contrary, **having-to-live** is getting power, skills and possessions to enable you impact the world or contribute to harmonized growth.

LIVING TO HAVE

"HAPPINESS for a reason is just another form of misery
because the reason can be taken away from us at any time."
– Deepak Chopra

Kenny had only used his phone for three months when the phone company released a 'latest' version. Apart from the colour and shape, the 'latest' version has no functional difference from the one Kenny already has. Kenny does not need the 'latest' phone for any new function that cannot be done by the three-month-old phone. Yet, he desperately desires the trending phone in order to be admired or to feel better than others. So, Kenny set his life to having trending gadgets, wears, trips, houses, status, jobs and other possessions, instead of relating with them as relevant means to his life's purpose.[16]

Fear of lacking resources begets two reactions: focus on personal survival and pleasure, or work for common good. The desire for personal survival comes to us impulsively, driving us to amass resources for personal survival before considering other people or environment. So, we **use** people, objects and indiscriminate careers for increasing personal security and pleasure, and live in constant fear of losing recognition, money, loyalty and resources for material happiness. Gradually, we become predators, heartless mercenaries, or indifferent robots trying to justify working against our responsible nature. Yet, choosing to work for common good after careful thoughts or developed habits enables growth, harmony and internal happiness.

b. HAVING TO LIVE

"Living is relating with humans, animals and environment for
their highest possible growth and right-use in the society."
– Restartnaija

Since growing up till she began working as a nurse, Amanda had observed the scourge of HIV/Aids around her and dedicated herself to tackle it. She studied and designed a software for enlightening and guiding people about the disease. Needing to reach more people, she bought powerful cameras, laptops, projectors and other gadgets, and continued the project until other people supported her. So, the more sponsorship she got, the more she improved herself for greater impact through research, outreach and medical equipment. Amanda prioritized her social impact, and considered having

---

[16] Chukwunwike Enekwechi, "when 'living-to-have' overtakes having to live, we suffer" in *Restartnaija. https://restartnaija.com/2019/02/12/when-living-to-have-overtakes-having-to-live-we-suffer/* retrieved 24/03/19

associates and materials as enabling companions for her life's purpose.[17] And with every self-development or social impact, she experiences more fulfilment as a socially-responsible being.

Having to live can be summarized in two questions:
1. What is the highest this person(s), animal, plant, thing or environment can become to positively impact the society?
2. How can I SUSTAINABLY ASSIST them become that and to make that social impact?

Using *'sustainably'* implies sustenance for continuity. So, in the course of assisting others, you develop and sustain yourself for better impact. The first consideration is impact, then sustenance through monetization of your assistance to other people or element's development and functionality. The difference between living-to-have and having-to-live is in the individual's primary intention either to get personal security and pleasure, or to make positive impact. While adherents of living-to-have only pursue projects for material happiness through personal security and pleasure, advocates of having-to-live pursue projects for social impact despite the certainty or uncertainty of reward. They do not hate wealth, they just have contentment. Contentment is not the absence of ambition, hatred of wealth and pleasure or love of mediocrity and pain. Instead, it is a demand for power, skills, resources or wealth based on your desire to be productive and socially responsible.[18]

Adherents of living-to-have adopt prosecutor's judgmental moods in the society to quickly blame people and justify their indifference. They make descriptive and shallow judgments on social issues with comments like: 'that's nice', 'that's bad', 'they are lazy, dumb, criminals, etc.' While adherents of having-to-live adopt health-workers' diagnostic and interventional disposition for discovering and addressing root-causes of social issues. They make committed and empathetic remarks like: how do we improve this good, or how do we control that threat. This is the disposition that guarantees our relevance and fulfilment in the society. We can relate with humans and environment for harmonized growth by reporting, advocacy, occasional social/material support or full-time devoted involvement.

---

[17] Chukwunwike Enekwechi, "when 'living-to-have' overtakes having to live, we suffer" in *Restartnaija*. https://restartnaija.com/2019/02/12/when-living-to-have-overtakes-having-to-live-we-suffer/ retrieved 24/03/19
[18] Chukwunwike Enekwechi, "Leading a family beyond financial security to fulfilment" in *Restartnaija,* 7th May, 2019. https://restartnaija.com/2019/05/07/leading-family-beyond-finance/ retrieved, 24th June, 2019.

In conclusion, man is on earth to assist nature in harmonizing growth in the world. Man does this by developing himself and relating with other humans, animals and objects for their highest possible development and right-use in the society. This means using resources to support growth and harmony, and to eliminate threats to them. Thus, Dalai Lama insists "Today more than ever before, life must be characterized by a sense of universal responsibility, not only nation to nation and human to human but also human to other forms of life."

"You are not here merely to make a living. You are here in order to enable the world to live more amply, with greater vision, with a finer spirit of hope and achievement. You are here to enrich the world, and to impoverish yourself if you forget the errand."
– Woodrow Wilson

Chapter 2

WHO BENEFITS FROM YOUR HAVING TO LIVE?

Scale of preference is an economic term for checking what we value more in given circumstances or among several options. This scale is also used to determine the preferred object for which we would likely sacrifice other things. A person who likes apples may give up a bigger bunch of banana for just one apple. A man who loves his wife more may rescue her first from a burning house before his own mother. A person who loves God *(or an idea of God)* may sacrifice his own comfort, family, pleasure and other things for *"God's command"*. And a person who staunchly values his personal or family's comfort above everything may not mind sacrificing a whole country or continent's wellbeing for his family's comfort. Depending on their influences and level of enlightenment, people can sacrifice many things for various passions, desires, objects or convictions.

In the previous chapter, we noted that the purpose of man's life is to develop and use his potentials and resources to enable growth and harmony in the world. The noblest disposition in harmonizing growth is devoting yourself to a purpose, instead of supporting randomly. Since devotion is the highest and most noble stage of living, it is important to define the people or things for who we are devoting our life. Malcolm X insists that if you don't stand for something you will fall for anything. And until you find something you are eager to die for, you are not living for anything.

<u>What type of benefits can we provide?</u>

Before identifying your life's major beneficiary, it is vital to distinguish the type of benefit implied. We consider things to be beneficial when they address our needs or contribute to our material or internal happiness. Hence, the benefits we provide are the products and services we produce from which people derive material and/or internal happiness. Productivity is the true expression of responsibility and reason, and the major testament of your living after death. Productivity can be categorized into two groups: material and nonmaterial production.

Material production: refers to the physical products humans develop from natural resources (minerals and agricultural harvests) to directly or indirectly satisfy human needs. They come from applying scientific knowledge on raw or processed natural resources through experiments and fabrications. They include food, drugs, houses, machines, clothes, books, gadgets, weapons, vehicles, fuel and all the components used for making them. Three stages in material production include primary production for extracting the crude natural resources; secondary production for processing the extracted resources to become useful items; and tertiary production for distributing the commodities to the people who demand or need it.

Nonmaterial production: are the intellectual, emotional, social and physical services we render to directly or indirectly satisfy human needs. They manifest in our efforts to discover, develop and utilize our various capacities for rendering specific services. Nonmaterial productions include production, distribution and use of ideas, knowledge, music, stories, drama, companionship, leadership, skills, social order, law, sports, recognition, intimacy, beauty and arts. The most important nonmaterial production is learning and guiding people to use their potentials and resources for happiness. Social education, which responds to our responsible nature, forms the foundation for scientific and commercial growth.

Both material and nonmaterial productivity complement each other. Makers of nonmaterial property need material products for testing, producing and sharing their productivity. For instance, musicians (song producers) need musical instruments, books, recorder and transmitter to produce and share music; researchers (knowledge producers) require research equipment, writing materials, printers and object of research to produce and share knowledge about what they research. Doctors use tools from engineers, drugs from pharmacists and medical knowledge from health researchers to provide healthcare. Likewise, makers of material property require nonmaterial products to motivate and direct their production, distribution and right-use of material products. Car makers need scientific research, tests, domestic services, adverts, social influence, legal/financial counsel and other nonmaterial products for sustenance. Yet, having natural resources is primary to productivity, since they form the foundation upon which ideas and items are developed, transmitted and sustained.

To know who benefits from our living, we consider who obtains material or nonmaterial resources for material or internal happiness from our productivity. Is it God, our family, country or humanity?

a. GOD
Can I focus on serving God to forget about the world?

A smart preacher distinguished the donation or service rendered to the poor from those rendered to God through churches. The preacher explained that giving to the poor meant giving to ordinary man who cannot bless or pay you back. But giving to the church meant giving to God himself who will bless and pay back with wealth on earth and happiness in heaven.[19] So, some people deem it wiser to seek material and internal happiness by channelling their productive benefits to God through religion.

Yet, some of the efforts to *'serve God'* contradict the natural principles of growth and harmony. Many terrorists pray and profess their love and service to God before slaughtering, shooting or bombing people. Some religious people neglect social needs, oppress or directly exploit others while gathering resources for *'serving God'*. These claims of serving God become doubtful in religious areas with high levels of social discrimination, poverty, violence, indifference and injustice.

Measuring the effects of our service to God
God is not a physical object we know by physical evidence, but an entity people accept by faith based on the wonders of nature. Measuring effects of our service to God follows from observing and aligning our services to the principles of nature, which are **GROWTH** and **HARMONY**. Thus, human actions align with God's wish when they enable social growth and harmony. Over time, people developed religions from divine experiences and beliefs, to direct humans to fulfilment. Presently, religion is not directly or scientifically linked to producing material items for security and pleasure. Instead, it provides means for internal happiness by motivating and directing people to discover, develop and use their potentials and resources for positive social impact.

Without defining the expected effects of serving God many absurdities are passed on to devout but naïve believers. Some sincerely naïve people

---

[19] Chukwunwike Enekwechi, "why give money to the church? Justification for church donations in the new era" in *Restartnaija,* 25th September, 2018. https://restartnaija.com/2018/09/25/why-give-church-justify-church-donations/ retrieved, 24th January, 2019.

execute absurd and often barbaric commands passed on to them as God's wish. In reference to such enthusiasts, Martin Luther King insists that "nothing in the world is more dangerous than sincere ignorance". Some paradigms that have been commonly used for measuring religions' impacts on the society include:

Religious expansion and global reach: As a member of a religion, you can be convinced that God wants you to spread your religion across the world. And that evil persists because you have not spread your religion or denomination to the whole world. Thus, you eagerly devote your resources to spread the religion globally as life's purpose and contribution for perfecting the world. Hoping that you can only improve the world by spreading religion, you can forget the goal (harmonious growth) while focusing on the means (spreading your religion). Being distracted from the main goal, you are tempted to apply methods of spreading religion that exploit, discriminate, neglect or directly oppress people. In this case, religion becomes a threat to harmonized growth, instead of support. Yet, you can direct your religion to enable human capacity development for productivity and social responsibility. Your search for internal happiness through religious expansion may be useless unless you direct it to providing means of fulfilment for humanity.

Worth, size and beauty of religious structures: Our imperfections often make us attach ourselves to external objects that seem better. If someone mocks our shortness or weakness, we flaunt our brother's height and strength as consolation or defence.[20] So, we make sacrifices to fortify and flaunt external objects or personalities as excuses or consolation for our imperfections. Likewise, you may devote resources to building religions' physical and corporate structures as your goal in life. Yet, the human and material resources for these structures often come from coded social exploitation. After contributing to religious structures to obtain fulfilment, we still witness the growing material and internal unhappiness in our societies. We still feel the violence, hatred, bitterness, crime, loneliness, depression, injustice and attack on harmonized growth in our environment.

By contributing to religious structures, you may briefly escape the sorrow, boredom and drowning emptiness of life. Yet, commitment to religious structures does not truly defend you from the assault of guilt and void of empty lives for neglecting social growth and harmony. Instead, you struggle to defend the choice of neglecting social responsibilities for religious structures. Finally, the structures become abandoned monuments

---

[20] Chukwunwike Enekwechi, "redirecting religious structures for productivity in Africa" in *Restartnaija,* 23rd April 2019. https://restartnaija.com/2019/04/23/redirect-religious-structures/ retrieved 29th April, 2019.

since they lacked elements of positive social impact.

Dramatic prayers, miracles and blissful worship: The current focus on planning, working, competing and surviving has a hypnotic effect on us. We gradually lose our humanity while becoming rigid and unthinking robots installed in factories, industries, offices and institutions. Despite these strides, we seem unable to solve all the problems emerging from our efforts to demonstrate super-power. In this robotic desert of modernism, we crave a touch of humanity and some connection with our origin. Religion provides avenues for us to feel a connection with the divine, manifest divine powers, direction or purpose. Through religious activities, we connect with people, feel heavenly bliss, consolation, life-direction, creative inspirations, motivational assurances (faith) and maybe, physical miracles.

Sometimes, these religiously blissful feelings do not provide the sustained internal happiness we seek, especially in unjust societies. We notice that they briefly console us or mask the social issues, until we direct them to material/nonmaterial productivity and social responsibility. It is possible to join in religious piety, rituals or miracles and still be wicked, unproductive, socially irresponsible and opposed to harmonized growth. If they do not lead to positive social impact, dramatic prayers and outward miracles may never ensure sustainable happiness. Thus, Mahatma Gandhi insists that 'to give pleasure to a single heart by a single act is better than a thousand heads bowing in prayer.'

Sustainable impact on humanity: *Who is more important to the society: a crippled but efficient programmer or a full-bodied wicked or lazy man?* Our world seem focused on external manifestations above the internal miracle of human transformation. Some clerics are praised for healing the cripple, curing the sick and bringing economic fortune. Only few people are recognized for enlightening the ignorant, rehabilitating the damaged and abused, motivating the lazy and discouraged, enabling the incompetent for productivity and humanizing the wicked. Yet, some people dedicate themselves to serving God by providing means for human capacity development towards positive social impact. They establish or support schools, hospitals, homes, pressure groups and schemes for social impact. In their nonphysical productivity they console, encourage and direct humans to social justice and truth for harmonized growth. Instead of waiting for miracles that are ungeneralizable for serving more people, they sponsor researches and legislative bills. They focus on internal miracle of transforming crude or damaged humans to productive and socially responsible beings.

Transforming human beings to productive and socially responsible beings is the greatest job, mission or miracle on earth. Transformed human beings convert deserts to cities, trees to medicine, woods, arts and stones to houses, mineral resources to human goods, human gathering to loving relationships and human resources to productive union/industry. But untransformed people turn cities to ruins, lives to death, joy to pain, peace to war/terror, relationships to chaos, natural resources to elements for oppression. Untransformed humans take advantage of social problems, not to solve the problem, but to exploit the problem for their gain. *E.g. a pharmacist who causes the spread of deadly diseases or addictions so that he can sell more drugs, or arms dealers who cause wars to sell weapons.*

> *Each religion of God is originally a source of rapid material and moral progress for mankind. However over time, like all things, it will slowly begin to decline and eventually lose its original influence and beauty, and is then in need of renewal.[21] "In truth, religion is a radiant light and an impregnable stronghold for the protection and welfare of the peoples of the world. For the fear of God impelleth man to hold fast to that which is good, and shun all evil. Should the lamp of religion be obscured, chaos and confusion will ensue, and the lights of fairness and justice, of tranquillity and peace cease to shine. Unto this will bear witness every man of true understanding." -*
> *Baha'u'llah*

A religion that works for you in bringing material happiness but does not work on you to be productive and socially responsible is not a true religion, but a social club, an occult group or a magical illusion. And until you see him in nature, environment and human beings, God remains an idea in your head, not a reality in your life. – Restartnaija

b. YOUR FAMILY
Can you always protect them?

The statement 'family is everything' emphasizes the importance of family for your happiness in life. Strictly speaking, family refers to those who share your immediate bloodline. But by association, it includes trusted friends and allies. These are the people with whom you share affections, interests, goals, memories and sources of happiness. They reflect your life efforts as extensions of yourself. They satisfy your need to be valued, to belong somewhere and relate with somebody by nature or destiny. With them, you feel unconditionally accepted, supported, advised and protected as a person,

---

[21] http://oneglobalfaith.org/for-the-curious/spirituality-without-religion/?gclid=Cj0KCQjw5fDWBRDaARIsAA5uWTjKqydQOr2bzy7DygFXISe6qhFcdWUHlXtP1M7oAwCEh1A5EOvJ6YsaAuONEALw_wcB

not just a tool for their material benefit. They are hopeful and proud for your growth, disappointed for your failure, and will make personal sacrifices to lift you up.

Because of our affection for them, we are willing to make sacrifices for their happiness. Yet, our understanding of the difference between material and internal happiness influences the category of benefit we seek for them. Following their basic instinct for material happiness, lions and other animals kill each other for their family's safety or pleasure. If you are not family, you are an enemy to destroy, prey to eat or nonsense to ignore. The difference between animal and human reaction to resources for material happiness is that while animals can only fight for them as final goals, humans can reason and dialogue to use them for internal happiness. The ability to get internal happiness from dialogue depends on the people's enlightenment about using material and nonmaterial resources.

When you solely focus on material happiness for your family, you can steal, kill and support unjust institutions without considering its effects on others. Thus, you obstruct harmonized growth, and the society becomes more dangerous to you who contribute, benefit or ignore their pain. Also, your family members for whom you support unjust social systems can oppose the unjust system, reject its benefits, become spoilt by pleasure or harmed by the human-brutes created by the system.

But if you primarily desire internal happiness for your family, you become socially responsible in using resources for self-development and harmonized growth. Then, you can direct family and friends to use resources to obtain fulfilment through productivity and social responsibility. If the sacrifice for your family does not help them obtain internal happiness, it becomes a prison of excuses from living. And if providing for your family alone is your main source of happiness in life, you become depressed and suicidal if they die or abandon you. But if you integrate them in your journey to fulfilment through social impact, even when they die, you contribute more to honour their memories.

c. YOUR COUNTRY

The inclination to narrow our lives' benefits to ourselves and our families can extend to our countries as closer allies in seeking happiness. If your country is secure and comfortable, you and your loved ones can hope to be secured and happy. So, we organize our countries to consistently obtain resources for comfort, security, entertainment, education, industry and prosperity. Successfully organizing a country for these benefits endears us to the country, such that we defend and contribute to it. And by contributing to our countrymen's safety and increased pleasure, we hope to gain not only material happiness, but also internal happiness.

Sometimes, efforts and success in providing security and pleasure for your countrymen fail to satisfy your hunger for internal happiness. You get relevance and fulfilment from overcoming real challenges to harmonized growth by helping those who **TRULY** need it, not just creating consumerist challenges for material happiness. It is difficult to get fulfilment from increasing security and pleasure for overfed, entitled and wasteful countrymen. It becomes worse when the resources come from exploiting other countries through unjust social structures, institutions and networks.

By only focusing on your countries' material happiness, even at other regions' detriment, your national life becomes a passionless and boring cycle between school, job, compensatory entertainment and house till death. In such consumerist disposition, you lose focus of the real-life challenges to conquer for relevance and internal happiness. Without overcoming real challenges to fill the emptiness in your life, you seek fun in ignoble dares or brutish challenges like death-race. This cycle typifies a network of coldblooded predators or robots programmed for consumerism at all cost. Eventually, you feel your descent into the lonely pit of perpetual obscurity and irrelevance to humanity. And when you die, fellow consumerist countrymen replace and forget you after few hours, few weeks for friends or few months for family. And in cases of possible whistle-blowing, you become a scapegoat or loose end they have to tie to sustain their greed and sanctimonious appearance to the world.

d. HUMANITY,
Can you care for the whole world?
"Our true nationality is MANKIND" - H. G. Wells

Different clubs in a football league, like La Liga, have presidents, managers, coaches, doctors, scouts, analysts, lobbyists, lawyers, agents, security, domestic staff, engineers and players like goalkeepers, strikers, defenders, midfielders or wingers. Nobody can do all the club's work alone. But by diligently and loyally performing your task, you contribute to the club's network for everyone's efficiency and happiness. Despite your club-loyalty, you respect other clubs whose existence and collaboration sustain the game, with whom you trade players, coaches and staff, and who provide the healthy challenge you need for developing yourself. Despite being in specific sections as country, region or race, our common humanity is broad, interlinked and interdependent. Humanity is not just me, you and the people we know, or people alive now. It includes the dead, whose memories, discoveries and institutions guide us, and the unborn, who will utilize and honour our legacies.

Since the human rights declaration, many people formally disapprove various forms of discrimination: racial, religious, gender or class. Instead, they approve common good as the measure and aim of good life and main source of true happiness. Great musicians, politicians, preachers, scientists, scholars, innovators, philanthropists and celebrities align themselves to serving humanity through their works. Thus, the intended beneficiaries of their efforts are not just themselves, their families, friends, religion, country or continent, but humanity. Yet, taking common good as the measure of good life confuses us on how to do good for everybody. Can anybody or action satisfy the whole of humanity without having critiques, opponents or losses?

Common good is a condition whereby a policy or innovation benefits majority of the society. Majority is used because it is almost impossible for everybody in a society to support or feel equally favoured by any policy, innovation or action. This raises questions on tyranny of the majority and its oppression of minority. What if a policy that benefits a certain majority steadily oppresses a particular minority? Is it still service to humanity and common good to continue with such policies since many people are comfortable with it against the minority that are perpetually oppressed by it?

A majority may be comfortable with such policies, if they are socially conditioned to focus on material or animal happiness. Hence, such people will choose gathering and using products and services only for their physical pleasure and security. They eagerly join and defend the comfortable majority so as to sustain resources for their animal happiness. Then, they miss the fundamental role of harmonizing growth in the world as the source of true happiness. From losing true happiness, they indirectly create beasts from the neglected minority who will terrorize their fake peace and burnt consciences.

Contrarily, socially enlightened persons desiring true happiness seek relating with humans for their full development, productivity and happiness. Despite belonging to specific locations as citizens, they contribute to harmonized growth through humanity's development and productivity. They know that developing and productively engaging more people according to their various capacities and locations enriches our world. To them, humans are not just heartless and cruel competitors, but potential collaborators to be influenced to develop and utilize their potentials to support responsible productivity and internal happiness. Their goal is a system where everybody fully develops and utilizes his potentials for positive social impact, dignity and sustenance.

Common good or serving humanity is not supplying all the resources people demand for material happiness like entertainment and luxury possessions. Most of the world's crises result from focusing on material/animal happiness while neglecting true happiness. Instead, common good is providing the resources humans require to develop and utilize their potentials for social impact, dignity and sustenance. It is not just providing food, cloth, shelter and entertainment for poor, homeless and deprived people, but chance for them to discover, develop and use their potentials for positive social impact, dignity and sustenance.

Working for common good is not like trying to fill empty containers and hope they retain the content. Instead, it is like lighting a candle to enable the candle to ignite other candles. It is not trying to fill people's insatiable desire for pleasure, but empowering people to become more productive in order to empower other people for increased productivity. Thus, the highest you can do to achieve harmonized growth is to create a social structure that enables people's development and productivity.

"We cannot help but believe that the old hatreds shall someday pass, that the lines of tribes shall soon dissolve, that as the world grows smaller our common humanity shall reveal itself, and that America must play its role in ushering in a new era of peace."
– Barack Obama

Chapter 3

REDEFINE YOUR PURPOSE

Lock your target

After hearing about the tastiness of antelope meat, Paul decided to hunt. He found some bullets in his grandfather's house. After inspecting the bullets, he chose the gun that can hold and fire those bullets and hunted consistently for six hours before catching two antelopes. Like hunting specific animals, fulfilment requires defining your target, its bullet and specific gun. Your target is your purpose or your intended impact in the world, your bullets are your character, knowledge, skills and possessions, and your gun is your group of collaborators in fulfilling your defined purpose.[22]

*"Everyone has his own specific vocation or mission in life;
everyone must carry out a concrete assignment that demands
fulfilment. Therein he cannot be replaced nor can his life be
repeated, thus, everyone's task is unique as his specific
opportunity to implement it."*
– Viktor Frankl.

Game of thrones is an epic movie that portrayed the medieval era with strict social gap between kings, lords and their ladies, commoners and slaves. At the time when King Robb Stark was fighting a war to avenge his father, he saw a beautiful lady, Talisa Magyar from Volantis, who was

---

[22] Chukwunwike Enekwechi, "Fulfilling your mission in Nigeria before running away" in *Restartnaija,* 25th January 2018. https://restartnaija.com/2018/01/25/fulfilling-your-mission-in-nigeria/ retrieved 30th March, 2019.

treating the sick and wounded soldiers in her blood-stained clothes. After some interactions and mutual admiration, King Robb became close to the Lady Talisa. One night when King Robb was pondering between riding south to avenge his father and riding north to secure his home, Lady Talisa came along. They discussed as follows:

Lady Talisa: What kind of king do you want to be?

King Robb: I don't know…, the good kind. Most kings grew up as princes, they spend their whole lives preparing to be king. I was raised to be Lord of Winterfell.

Lady Talisa: I was raised to be a proper little lady, to play the harp and dance the latest dance and recite Valerian poetry.

King Robb: how did you go from reciting Valerian poetry to sawing off men's feet and treating sick people and soldiers in battlefields?

Lady Talisa: When I was 12, my mother and father went to a wedding. Weddings in Volantis last for days, you know. And they left me with my little brother. The second afternoon they were gone was the hottest day in the three year summer. We couldn't bear to be inside the heat, so we ran down to the ruin (village stream). Every child in Volantis was in the ruin that day. The rich, the poor, we were all there naked, screaming, racing to the little islands. Drummers were playing drums in the east bank. I was treading water, talking to a friend, when I realized I haven't seen my brother. I called his name then I started screaming his name. And then I saw him floating face down, my heart just stopped. I was… (sighs) I dragged him from the water, my friend helped me I think. I don't even remember. He was so little and we pulled him over the river bank. And I screamed at him, and I shook him, and he was dead…, just dead. A man ran over. He had a fish tattooed on his face. In Volantis, the slaves have tattoos, so you know **what** they are without having to talk to them. And this man worked in a fishing boat (that's why he had a fish tattooed on his face). And he pushed me out of the way. You have to understand, for a slave to push a highborn girl, that's death for the man, a terrible death. But he pushed me out of the way, and started pressing on my brother's chest, again and again and again until my brother spat out half of the ruin and cried out. And the man cradled his head and told him to be calm.

I decided two things that day: I would not waste my years planning and learning new dances and masquerades with the other noble ladies, and that when I become of age, I will never live in a slave city again.[23]

Oscar Wilde states that "most people are other people. Their thoughts are someone else's opinions, their lives a mimicry, their passions a quotation." Internal happiness has continuously eluded many of us because we failed to discover ourselves and our specific life-purposes as we strive to conform to other people's ideas about us. As rational and creative beings, we are responsible for harmonizing growth in the world. But since we cannot individually harmonize everything at once, we form sections for it, just like football clubs have different but interlinked individuals. By coming into the club of life at birth, nature has confidently deposited unique potentials in each person. Yet, each person has to find his particular role in harmonizing growth in the world in order to attain internal happiness.

Finding your specific role in harmonizing growth in the world is a most difficult but most rewarding enterprise in life. Mark Twain insists there are two days in a person's life: the day he is born and the day he discovers why. Without discovering your life's purpose, you will remain a robot or tool for someone or something that compensates you with money, pleasure or recognition. Or you internally struggle to defend your social irresponsibility with the premise of doing what makes you happy (animal happiness), or condemning the society for not deserving your responsibility. But when you find your specific role in harmonizing growth, your life becomes meaningful, passionate, unique and valuable. Three areas to examine when searching for your purpose or role in harmonizing growth in the world are your **passion or dream**, your **talent** or **disposition** and your **location of influence**.

YOUR SOCIAL PASSION or DREAM
"Every child is an artist. The problem is how to remain an artist once we grow up" –
Pablo Picasso

Getting pregnant, bearing a baby and nurturing him to become socially responsible is exciting. After relating with a man, a woman conceives and carries a child in her womb for several months. She avoids some activities, foods and drugs to protect the unborn child from possible harm. Also, she begins special dieting, exercises, studies, shopping and environmental preparations to support the unborn child until birth. After birth, the mother introduces the baby to the world and passionately cares, nurtures, protects

---

[23] *Game of Thrones*, by David Benioff and D. B Weiss Season 2, episode 8.

and educates her child till he matures to become productive and socially responsible. Mothers develop themselves, take risks and sacrifice their comforts to protect, guide and nurture their babies. A mother can jump into a burning house to save her baby. Even single mothers insist that intending suitors must adopt their babies or forget the marriage.

Like conceiving babies by relating with men, we conceive dreams and ideas of a better world while relating with our imperfect world. We all want to improve, impact or change the world, especially the evil imperfections we felt most. As mothers protect their babies, if we protect and nurture our dreams till birth and maturity, they grow to influence our lives, decisions, careers and impacts in the world. But if we get distracted by cultures of fear, greed or indifference, our dream lies silent in us. It does not just die in us, it simply becomes a passive *resident,* instead of active *president* of our lives. For despite impulses to flee from imperfections, our rational instinct of creativity and responsibility urges us to intervene. At this point we are more concerned about the impact to make in the society, than the title it gives us or the profession we use for it. So, our passions and dispositions sound more like:

I want to *impart* productive and socially responsible knowledge, not just to be a lecturer, teacher, researcher, writer, publisher, journalist or newscaster;

I want to *support* people's spiritual direction, motivation and wellbeing for productivity and social responsibility, not just to be a priest, pastor or clergy;

I want to *enthrone* social justice, instead of I want to be a lawyer, judge or policeman;

I want to *ensure* good health, instead of I want to be a doctor, nurse, nutritionist or health worker;

I want to *develop* clean, available and affordable medications, instead of I want to be a pharmacist;

I want to *ensure* security, instead of I want to be a defence personnel in military, ideological, medical, biological, genetic, chemical, radiation or cyber threats, terrorist networks and predatory drug companies and cartels;

I want to *curb* waste of resources and harmonize productivity, instead of I want to be an economist;

I want to *build* beautiful/helpful structures and machines, instead of I want to be an engineer;

I want to *entertain, refresh and direct* people for productivity and social responsibility, not just I want to be an actor, musician, comedian, sportsman, writer, director, etc.

I want to *inspire* people to develop productive self-esteem, not just to be artist, model or beautician;

I want to ***cloth and beautify*** people, not just I want to be a fashion designer or tailor;

I want to ***facilitate*** productive communication in the world, instead of I want to be an IT specialist;

I want to ***ensure food security***, instead of I want to be a farmer or food businessman;

I want to ***empower*** people for productivity, not I want to be a social entrepreneur or philanthropist;

I want to ***enable*** proper social administration for responsible productivity, instead of I want to be a politician or activist;

I want to ***connect*** quality producers to right consumers, not just I want to be a marketer;

I want to ***motivate*** socially responsible endeavours with adequate recognition or publicity, not just I want to be a host, hype-man, publicist or advertiser.

When you decide on the impact to make in the society, it becomes clearer to choose between careers as tools for your impact according to the need and place. When you identify health as your impact, you can then choose from nursing, health-education, physiotherapy, lab-science, medicine, surgery or others depending on the area and need. But if you rigidly insist on a particular career not considering social need, you mentally limit your capacity to intervene in cases outside the career. Professions and careers are tools from which you choose how to meet your target impact or purpose.

The purpose-first-mentality directs careers as means for impact, but career-first-mentality limits the individuals' focus on impact. Your social purpose does not end with your chosen career, otherwise you become useless to the world after retiring from football, politics, medical practice or other careers. Second, you will lack zeal to make any social impact if you do not get the specific career. Last, without defining your social purpose before career, you could be distracted to abuse the career when you get it.

To discover your social passion or dream, you play, laugh, explore, encounter and engage the world and its peoples for happiness. In playing and encountering the world, you encounter limitations, evils and challenges that obstruct happiness for you and other people. You witness challenges like diseases, wars, poverty, injustice, crimes, bitterness and emptiness of life. Some challenges have deeper effects in some people than in others.

To live purposefully and victoriously, you dedicate yourself to overcoming the particular challenges that scare or affect you the most, otherwise you keep running, living in denial and being a cowardly deserter all your life. You do not find your social passion or dream by hiding in a comfortable house, city, acquired or inherited luxury, prophecy or parental dictates. As a lady associates with a strong man to get pregnant, you engage the imperfect and rough world to find your social purpose from its impressions. Your destiny is not a given, you discover it and work on it, even if you start alone without some expert template. Thus, Mark Zuckerberg notes that "ideas don't come out fully formed, they develop as you begin working on them." And the greatest mistake you can make is to do nothing because you fear you will make mistakes, fail, suffer, only do little or are not qualified to try. Remember there's no such thing as unrealistic goal, just unrealistic time frames.[24]

> *"The whole secret of a successful life is to find out what*
> *is one's destiny to do, and then do it."*
> – Henry Ford

YOUR TALENTS AND SPECIFIC DISPOSITIONS

"Zaldrizes buzdari iksos daor" – A dragon is not a slave
"Your gifts, powers and talents are not your toys, they are collaborators to your purpose."
– Restartnaija

After using her dragons to liberate slaves and captives in slave-cities of Meryn and slaver's bay, the dragon-queen, Daenerys Targaryen, spoke to King Jon Snow about the dynamics of having dragons:

> *"…A dragon is not a slave. They were terrifying, extraordinary, they filled people with wonder and awe; and we locked them in here. They wasted away, they grew small, and we grew small as well. We weren't extraordinary without them, we were just ordinary like everyone else."*[25]

Like having dragons for battle, each person has unique talents or dispositions for accomplishing their social purposes. Your talents and dispositions are nature's distinguishing gifts that enable you to follow and accomplish your purpose for the world. These gifts include skills in music, sports, arts, writing, fighting, fashion, teaching, producing or leading, and dispositions like intelligence, patience, tolerance, empathy, bravery, strategy, calculation, beauty, analytics, charisma or physical strength. Like feeding and training a dragon, you perfect these talents and dispositions through steady practice and learning. When you properly develop them, they make

---

[24] Donald J Trump
[25] Game of thrones, season 7 episode 7

you extraordinary, awesome, admirable and useful to fulfil your purpose. But without understanding that these talents are for accomplishing your purpose, you either misuse them for evil or neglect them to waste away. These skills, talents, professions, careers, powers, offices and awards are not life purposes in themselves. They are your undisputed and indispensable means to fulfilling your social dreams and purposes.

Realizing the importance of gifts and talents in fulfilling his social dreams, Paul David Hewson (Bono) states: "As a rock star, I have two instincts, I want to have fun, and I want to change the world. I have a chance to do both." Muhammed Ali used his boxing fame to preach against injustice, war crimes and exploitation. Many footballers like Cristiano Ronaldo and Kanu Nwankwo, musicians, actors, pageants and celebrities use their fame to fight racism, war and injustice, or to promote some noble causes in the society. Steve Harvey uses comedy to inspire safe and cordial relationship. Judge Lynn Toler uses her courtroom to educate and heal families. Jeremy Kyle uses his talk-show to unite families on truth and mercy; Michael Jackson, Albert Einstein used, and Didier Drogba, Oprah Winfrey and others use their gifts to influence the world.

It is not enough to be a good person with noble dreams and kind heart. You must find and develop your strength, discipline, talents, character and skills in order to confront obstacles to your social purpose. Otherwise, your good heart becomes useless and unable to effect positive change. A mother develops strengths or social links to confront threats to her child's security and wellbeing, otherwise she loses her baby.

"Know your strength, use it wisely, and one man will be
stronger than 10,000 men."
– Peter Baelish

YOUR LOCATION OF INFLUENCE

*We hold these to be true: that **all** men are equal,*
***all** men are free and **all** deserve a chance to pursue a full measure of happiness.*
- American declaration of independence

After discovering your social dream and developing your talents and dispositions for fulfilling it, the next step is knowing where to apply it. The world is our nation, humanity is our identity and global creativity with social responsibility is human route to common good. ***To attain full happiness, all men and all societies need both material and nonmaterial resources to be productive and socially responsible.*** Any part of the world lacking productivity and social responsibility is a setback to human progress and happiness. As marketers trade their goods where it is scarce, humans impact their social purposes where happiness is lacking. They direct their passions to provide material and nonmaterial resources for true happiness where it is lacking. The situation of material or internal happiness in your place of origin helps you decide whether you work **_IN_**, **_FOR_** or **_FROM_** your place of origin. Your place of origin refers to your historically established location of communal or ancestral settlement and heritage.

- **IN your place of origin**: Nobody chooses the family, community, society, race or ancestral settlement s/he is born into. Nature designedly assigns each person along with his potentials, dispositions and talents to different places in the world. Thus, being born into a specific society means being sent to be responsible for it, and to contribute to its full measure of happiness. Your opportunity for fulfilment lies in discovering and supplying resources for the type of happiness lacking in your place of origin. Whether they lack resources for internal happiness or the resources for material happiness, you get there to supply.

  You may be born into a society that is historically disorganized and deprived of their resources for productivity through political manipulations. People in such areas suffer and die in poverty, hunger, desperation, crimes, ignorance and avoidable diseases. With the lack of opportunity, people die with their untapped and undeveloped potentials and geniuses. Such deprivation can reduce your people to animal level of thinking, desperately fighting for survival or animal happiness, not creativity nor fulfilment. So, your society seems like caged gladiators or beasts fighting one another, instead of collaborating to free themselves and reorder their society for productivity. There, your work towards fulfilment becomes educating your society to reorder themselves for productivity. Your social education may require some creativity to enlighten and convince the disorganized people for social reorganization.

  On the other hand, you may feel lucky to be born into a society with abundant resources and products for material happiness. Yet, many people in such societies lack the internal happiness that comes from social responsibility and creativity. Your emptiness of internal happiness increases if the resources for sustaining your material happiness come from your people's exploitation of some oppressed parts of the world. Thus, your society becomes like hyenas holding and eating an antelope, even while it is still alive and standing. Then your role towards internal happiness increases from educating, persuading or conscientizing your people for responsible resource-management to making reparations by enabling productivity and social responsibility in the areas.

- **FROM your place of origin:** The ethical burden of being human imposes a responsibility not only for your place of origin, but for the world. When your society has built stable systems for material happiness, even without exploiting other people, you still desire national fulfilment from contributing to harmonized growth in the world. You desire the fulfilment from being relevant to both the unfulfilled and the materially deprived peoples of the world. Thus, your role involves canvassing support for extending material and nonmaterial resources for other societies to attain productivity and/or social responsibility, as a missionary, sponsor, journalist, aid-worker, researcher, policy-maker, etc. This requires readiness to counter opposition from individuals and groups that sustain and benefit from the exploitative status-quo.

- **FOR your place of origin:** due to insecurity, unproductivity, political crisis, natural disasters or other factors, some people migrate from their places of origin. Some naturalize in their places of exile, establish new families and adopt new mentalities or identities. Due to scary situations that caused the migration, you may try to abandon or erase links to your place of origin. Yet, after pretending to ignore your place of origin, you still listen and feel disturbed about its horrible condition. And you will be truly happy and proud if it is raised to glory, especially if you contributed to its rise. Thus, you can either respond smartly by blaming others to defend your cowardly inaction, or respond in greatness by committing to social intervention.

The first step in responding in greatness is to identify the causes of unproductivity in the place. ***For without material and nonmaterial productivity, no society can achieve social responsibility for solving problems, even if they truly want to solve their problems.*** To solve the problem of unproductivity, you identify its political, cultural, academic, environmental, legal and historical causes. You must study deep and understand properly, for "there is nothing more frightful than ignorance in action."[26] After identifying the root causes of unproductivity, you plan solutions and involve other people for implementation. You may not personally or singularly conduct the researches, but you can support others who are eager and capable for it.

Without deciding and impacting actual groups and locations that need your influence for true happiness, you may unknowingly be supporting oppressors, or supplying resources for animal happiness to an ungrateful, entitled and arrogant people. To fulfil your purpose, you must find your social passion, discover and develop your talents or gifts, and impact the location where your dream is most relevant.

WHY REDEFINE YOUR PURPOSE?

- **To know who you are:** People differ, and each person has his creative passions for the society and various dispositions for actualizing those passions. Finding the dream that responds to your desire for creativity and responsibility, and being yourself in a world that is constantly trying to make you something else is the greatest accomplishment.[27] Otherwise, you become so good at acting what you are expected to act, that you forget who you are in actuality.

- **To have a reason to live and die:** Death comes to us all at any time or place; but dying for nothing means wasting your life. Like a mother for her child, you need a noble reason to live, hope, endure, strive and sacrifice your comfort or even your life. Something noble must grow from your life's journey and efforts, or you would have lived and died for nothing. "Losing your way on a journey is unfortunate. But, losing your REASON for the journey is a fate

---

[26] Johann Wolfgang Von Goethe 1826, conferred from Antonio Frasconi, americanart.si.edu/artwork/there-is-nothing-more-frightful-than-ignorance-action-goethe-1826-series-great-ideas-western-man/

[27] Ralph Waldo Emerson, www.brainyquotes.com retrieved, 24th June, 2019.

more cruel."[28]

- **To have a focus and a legacy:** He who pursues too many things at once may never succeed in one thing. Redefining your purpose helps you focus your energies on an aspect of the society, where you can impact zealously. You can redefine and start over if you value your happiness.

- **To avoid unnecessary competitions:** the social media era has increased the level of unhealthy competition that increases depression. Many people fight to defeat others or to prove that they are happy by showing off and bragging about every real or fabricated acquisition or achievement. By redefining your purpose, you no longer strive to be the best on someone's measuring scale of success. You become different and continue improving to reach your purpose. For Ayn Rand, a creative man is motivated by the desire to make impact, not the desire to beat others.

Imagine narrating your life's journey to your real or adopted grandchildren towards the end of your life. In a reverse order, outline the story of your life from death to present, and highlight the steps you climbed and the challenges you overcame towards your social impacts and meaningful life. Everything you are doing now form the story of your victorious life over the challenges that scared you in life, or your cowardly defeated life running from the challenges that scared you in life. ***You can fight a lot of enemies and survive, but if you fight yourself, your passion or your destiny,*** you will always lose.[29] You will never be proud or happy with yourself or with your life of cowardice and constant denial.

---

[28] H G wells
[29] Yuri, in the movie *"Lord of war"* by Andrew Niccol, 2005.

Chapter 4

IDENTIFY AND DEVELOP YOUR TOOLS, TALENTS AND CHARACTER

Sharpening your bullets or training your dragons

Can you remember the last time you made a sincere and firm resolution about stopping something or starting something? Maybe on New Year eve when you resolve to control your urge for gambling and to invest wisely; after admiring some models and resolve to work out daily for thirty minutes; on your wedding day when you sincerely resolve to be faithful to your spouse; after the conflict when you decide to devote at least twenty minutes daily to your family; on the induction or inauguration day when you fervently resolve to observe best practice as an officer, practitioner or politician; when you were caught cheating on your partner, breaking vows or indulging in terrible but secret addictions; during a car or plane crash when you promise to repent fifty times if you survive, *haha… gotcha!* It happens to us all. At each of these crossroads, we make sincere resolutions and truly intend to live through them. Unfortunately, we begin to **gradually** shift, compromise on what we forbade, over-procrastinate tasks, make excuses and finally forget them.

"If we want to direct our lives, we must take control of our consistent actions. It's not what we do once in a while that shapes our lives, but what we do consistently." – Tony Robbins

Humans are naturally good

Human beings are not born evil. By our transcendental nature, we are disposed to give and expect kindness, to protect others and identify with goodness. If you are walking through a corridor and overhear people who do not know you are around talking about how honest, kind and disciplined you are, you will feel very happy. You may try to identify them and treat them nicely on a later date. On the contrary, if you overheard them talking about how pretentious, wicked, lazy and corrupt you are, you will feel terrible, and either seek to confront, hurt or avoid them. Humans naturally identify with good despite their faults because goodness is ingrained in the depth of our being.

In the movie 24 hours, Jack Bauer spoke to Nina Myers about the slippery slope from little compromise to full-blown habitual vice and corruption: *"Nina, you can look the other way once and say it's no big deal, except it makes it easier for you to compromise the next time. And pretty soon, that's all you are doing, compromising, because you think that's how it is done. You know the guys I blew the whistle on, you think they were the bad guys? No. They are not the bad guys, they just compromised, ONCE."*

By their rationality, humans are disposed to desire and respond to kindness as agents of harmonizing growth in the world. Most of the tyrants, criminals, villains and cruel people began their life journeys with kind intentions and resolutions. However, their failures begin from gradual compromises on their resolutions until they acquire habitual corruption or wickedness. Thus, Friedrich Nietzsche insists that "it is not the strength, but the duration, of great sentiments that makes great men."

Factors that derail humans from social impact

All human virtues and vices can be traced to our reactions to- three basic emotions: love, fear and anger. When we love somebody or something, we desire to own them or see them grow; second, we fear losing them to anybody or thing; and third, we get angry if we lose them or if they are threatened, hurt or taken by other people, and this anger grows to become hatred. Our love for anything depends on our belief in their capacity to bring us security, pleasure or fulfilment. And the fear of losing them yields either basic or enlightened responses.

The basic response, which we share with animals, comes to us instinctively to choose sectional survival for ourselves and then our allies, and to see others as enemies or tools for our pleasure and survival. Moved by this instinct, we eagerly grab, secure or consume resources and products with greed or deceit. Also, we react to threat or loss of desired resources with violent emotions. Steadily responding with greed, deceit and violence to our fears is intended to satisfy our hunger for material happiness.

However, the enlightened response comes from a higher level of understanding, to take responsibility for harmonizing growth in the environment. Inspired by this motive, we cooperate with other people to develop and use our potentials and resources for common good. As responsible beings, success in improving life in our environment fills us with internal happiness. To consistently respond like this, we see, relate and build others as potential allies, not just tools to use or enemies to crush. Three ideals for checking your drift into basic response, and for ensuring collaboration with others for harmonious growth are *sincerity, generosity* and *modesty*.

IDEALS FOR ACHIEVING YOUR PURPOSE

After making computers, manufacturers install operating systems like windows or android as the foundations to support all future applications for the system. Without installing strong operating systems, other applications will continue malfunctioning until they crash the system. It is like planting trees on weak soil, or building skyscrapers on weak foundation. Sincerity, generosity and modesty are the foundational tools for actions towards responsible productivity and true happiness.

Sincerity
As long as we believe in absurdities, we shall continue to commit atrocities.
- Voltaire

Sincerity is living by truth, and truth is "to say of what is that it is, or of what is not that it is not."[30] It is the quality of being honest, true and real.[31] It includes absence of pretence, deceit or hypocrisy.[32] We differentiate between enabling and action sincerity.[33]

*** Enabling sincerity** is the verbal, written, sign, graphic or dramatized supply of true information to enable other people's decisions and actions for responsible productivity and true happiness. The opposite of enabling sincerity is lie or cover-up, which is mostly done for personal gains, escaping justice or pain. People suffer, die, go to jail or war because of other people's lies, cover-ups, silence and marketing deceptions. A problem with lies and cover-ups is that you keep lying to cover them, while

---

[30] Simon W. Blackburn, "Philosophy and logic" in *Britannica.*
https://www.britannica.com/topic/truth-philosophy-and-logic retrieved 6th January, 2019.
[31] http://www.yourdictionary.com/sincerity
[32] .https://www.google.com.ng/search?q=define+sincerity&oq=define+sincerity&aqs=chrome..69i57j
0l5.4283j1j1&sourceid=chrome&ie=UTF-8
[33] Chukwunwike Enekwechi, "The midwife leader: the leader Nigeria needs" in *Restartnaija,* 23rd March, 2018. https://restartnaija.com/2018/03/23/midwife-leader-leader-nigeria-needs/ retrieved 29th April, 2019.

decaying within.

    * **Action sincerity** is personal dedication to fulfil your words of commitment or agreement. Some people commit themselves in seemingly harmless pledges – **I WILL** call, support, read, come, give or do something – without intending or making efforts to do them. This attitude seems harmless until it becomes a habit, whereby your words lose meaning for people who have met you. It also affects your own ability to believe yourself about commitments.

<u>Requirements for sincerity</u>

Sincerity is living by truth, and truth is the highest medicine, healing or booster for human mind, and the most useful ingredient for social growth, harmony and true happiness. Like developing medicine, the process of getting truth is rigorous and requires specific dispositions from truth-seekers. Among the requirements for obtaining truth are:

- **Curiosity:** This is a strong desire to know about something.[34] It rises from a desire to understand and manage the world for our survival and happiness. Edward Denning insists that "It is good to do your best. But before then, you have to know what to do before doing your best." The burden of responsibility for our actions and the information we provide as enabling sincerity drives us to read, experiment and research thoroughly. Yet, responsibility guides you against reckless or extreme curiosity that violates people's privacy, for according to William Forrester, "the object of a question is to obtain information that matters to us, and not to others".

- **Humility:** This is the **readiness** to accept truth whenever it shows itself.[35] It requires internal freedom and openness to accept our failures and lack of absolute knowledge. We often listen to argue instead of listening to understand because we are rigidly attached to some beliefs, without evaluating them against our common humanity. Humility disposes you to seek and accept truth even in odd places and people like subordinates or children without simply appealing to authority. For truth does not depend on established authority or popularity of ideas, but in conformity of our statements with past, present or possible realities. The basic truth for social growth is that we are all humans, irrespective of race,

---

[34] Oxford Advanced Learner's Dictionary, International Student's Edition. S. V. curiosity
[35] Chukwunwike Enekwechi, "Political parties and the distraction from development in Nigeria" in *Restartnaija,* 14th August 2018. https://restartnaija.com/2018/08/14/political-parties-distraction-development-nigeria/ retrieved, 29th April, 2019.

class, privilege, faults, history, endowments, habits and beliefs, and we all desire true happiness.

- **Critical thinking:** The readiness to accept truth does not imply gullibility or absence of doubt and questions about claims of truth. As long as humans seek truth for happiness, there are people who will keep presenting falsities as routes to happiness. For Bertrand Russell, men are born ignorant, not stupid. They are made stupid by education (indoctrination). So, despite your readiness to accept the truth, you require critical thinking to examine various claims of truth. John Locke says that 'reading furnishes the mind only with materials of knowledge; it is thinking that makes what we read ours.' The abundance of evil in our world shows lack of thinking.

- **Discretion:** Being sincere does not also imply being talkative or stupid. Discretion helps you protect info that can expose innocent people, their names and affairs to harm. Giving up a victim's hideout to pursuant-kidnappers or armed robbers is not sincerity, but indiscretion. The armed robbers or kidnappers have no investment or legitimate right to that truth. Also, you protect people's delicate data and benign mistakes from gossips and societal witch-hunters.

- **Courage:** This is the ability to do something dangerous, or face pain or opposition, without showing fear.[36] It is a strong disposition of the mind to manage difficult or uncertain situations. Courage as a requirement for sincerity does not imply absence of fear in facing the consequences of truth, like lack or punishment. Instead, it is the belief that you will succeed when you confront and manage any circumstance resulting from standing by truth. This is the courage to believe and stand for the past, present and possible truths about your dreams, people, life, the world and your imaginations for life. Albert Einstein states, I'd rather be an OPTIMIST and a fool than a pessimist and right. For reality is incomplete. It grows from man's sincere and constant work.

Nobody is, or can be perfect… The element for greatness is sincere effort. Thus, sacrificing truth for expediency is the root of social injustice. – Restartnaija

---

[36] Oxford Advanced Learner's Dictionary, International Student's Edition. S. V. courage

Generosity

"In the name of the warrior, I charge you to be brave.
In the name of the father, I charge you to be just.
In the name of the mother I charge you to defend the innocent… Arise a knight."
- Sir Jaime Lannister knighting Brienne of Tarte

Generosity is the willingness to freely give care, time or possession for other people's good. It includes the readiness to help and to actualize your social dreams despite human and environmental obstacles. It is also being "kind in the way you treat other people and willing to see what is good about somebody or something."[37] The aim of generosity is to change the world to a place of true happiness or where all men are equal, free and have the chance to pursue true happiness. In unjust societies with legalized deprivation, generosity can be divided in two, namely palliative and liberation generosity.

PALLIATIVE generosity helps its recipients to cope in manmade exploitative situations by providing food, clothes, basic formal education, consolation, survivalist jobs and motivational speeches for personal survival. It responds to people's immediate needs in unjust situations, but may not provide resources for their liberation. It is like feeding or comforting a prisoner without freeing him from his bondages: cultural, political, ideological, economic, legal or behavioral. Though palliative generosity is important to sustain prisoners while they seek freedom, it is an insufficient response to bondages that deprive people of the chance to fully develop themselves for true happiness. Many aid agencies, NGOs and religious groups fall within this category to help victims of social injustice cope in their bondage.[38] Despite being an important form of generosity, it can be used to distract captives of social injustice from ever demanding or obtaining their freedom. To avoid being a source of distraction from people's freedom, you also prepare the recipients mentally for liberty or freedom.

LIBERATION generosity enables its recipients to demand and obtain freedom from cultural, political, economic, ideological and behavioral bondages. It includes socio-political education, movements and efforts for reorganizing unjust and unfavorable social structures, traditions, laws and orders. This is the most important form of generosity, as it aims to reorder social structures for people to develop and utilize their potentials and resources for productivity and true happiness. Despite being the most

---

[37] Oxford Advanced Learner's Dictionary, International Student's Edition. S. V. generosity, generous

[38] Chukwunwike Enekwechi, "The politics of charity and baseless motivational speeches" in *Restartnaija,* 7th October, 2017. https://restartnaija.com/2017/10/07/politics-of-charity-and-motivation/ retrieved 29th April, 2019.

important form of generosity, it needs palliative generosity to sustain people while they seek freedom. For liberation generosity takes more time, courage, research, education, planning and alliances before implementation.

Despite their difference, both palliative and liberation generosity are vital for harmonizing growth, and you can contribute in any as long as it does not obstruct the other.

Not all societies have strictly exploitative structures that need liberation generosity, yet every society has avenues for expressing generosity. Some societies have abundant material happiness, but lack resources and avenues for internal happiness. There is nobody so rich that he does not need anything from anybody to achieve or sustain happiness. Generosity is thus, consistency in intervening where material or internal happiness is lacking, especially against your fears, laziness, indifference, greed and desire for recognition. Through generosity, you activate people and their environment to support others for extending happiness. Some areas for impacting other forms of generosity include:

- **Justice as career:** Justice is "giving to each person what he deserves." As humans and parts of different societies, we all deserve resources for full happiness through productivity and social responsibility. Yet, political and environmental factors deprive some people of access to both material and nonmaterial resources for happiness. In response, some people form volunteer groups to extend material and nonmaterial resources for full happiness. Such groups allow you express your generosity, teach, write, donate and support people who truly need it.

- **Random help:** Different societies have agencies for different tasks in the society like health, security, environmental and emergency units. Yet some problems occur where and when agents are unable or unavailable to solve problems like accidents, disasters, social disorder or cases of stranded or unfortunate people. You express generosity in such areas by helping out, if you are attentive to your environment and not locked up in your little world.

- **Defence from physical, mental, emotional or social harm:** This involves defending innocent people, their reputation, courage and affairs from physical, verbal and emotional harm.

- **Daily business:** The current transactional mood of the society often conditions us to focus on what we earn, while withholding nonmaterial gifts we can give. Gestures like honest direction on products, care, appreciation and check-ups on clients contribute to their full happiness. So, Visvesvaraya insists that "to give real service, you must add something which cannot be bought or measured with money." In this case, generosity becomes the extra effort we add to increase the value of services and their capacity to provide full happiness.

- **Emotional generosity:** Mother Theresa says that the highest sickness of the modern age is not cancer or HIV, but the feeling of not being desired or loved. The modern-day individualism continues to frighten and isolate us from other people, resulting in loneliness and depression. It brings a siege mentality, where we think that everyone wants to exploit us, and that nobody cares. Experiences and reports about loss, neglect, cruelty and agony increase these fears. Though people seem distracted and uncaring, you must not wait to receive their impressions. Instead, you begin making impressions by empathizing with people, expect their success, listen to them, understand them, call, chat up, greet, celebrate and mourn with them.

<u>Requirement for true generosity</u>: anonymity

In this social media era where charity works are celebrated online, you may desire to be recognized or celebrated for your intervention. By giving into the desire for recognition, you unconsciously begin to require publicity before any social impact. Gradually, you start neglecting your dream for common good while focusing on trending, publicized and celebrated projects. Thus, millions of socially-deprived people remain neglected after few persons are publicized and dramatized for public show of palliative sympathy and philanthropy. However, these shows of sympathy do not address the structural causes of the problems. They just cuddle few hyped cases. To be truly generous, you contribute to readjusting the social structure to liberate people from the socio-political causes of their deprivations, without the intention of publicity.

Expecting internal happiness from publicizing your generosity is like expecting to be surprised after paying someone to organize a *'surprise'* appreciation party for you. The only thing that will surprise you is when the person runs away with your money without organizing the party. But as long as you paid for the party, you can never get the fulfilment of being truly surprised, loved, valued or appreciated. You know you are just doing a mechanistic business transaction for image laundering.

Generosity is the practical expression of love.
It is stewardship. – Restartnaija

Modesty

"As long as humans are unable and unwilling to recognize their destructive nature, they must be lost in it and therefore cannot attain proper self-identification." – Schoenstatt.
Virtue lies in the middle – Aristotle

Modesty is the steady choice of responsible approaches in relating with humans and environment for harmonized growth. It is the ability to control one's impulses, emotions and appetites. As humans with fragile bodies, insatiable appetites and raging desires, we want freedom to indulge our desires and impulses, and we hate restriction, pain and lack. Yet, without controlling both pleasant and unpleasant desires, we sooner or later meet horrible consequences. Modesty enables you seek better ways of resolving conflicts without being beastly, and better ways of engaging pleasure without being nasty. The mode of expressing modesty in pleasure differs from the mode of modesty in displeasure or pain.

<u>Modesty in pleasure:</u> we derive pleasure by interacting with the environment and humans, by playing, singing, dancing, storytelling, discussing, social gathering, working-together, procreating or eating. By doing these activities, we develop attachment for the activity, the feeling and/or the people involved. Pleasure can inspire and enable you to develop and use your potentials and resources for sustaining and increasing wellbeing.[39] Yet, when the attachment to pleasure activities, things or people obstructs your productivity or social responsibility, it becomes vicious. Then, it becomes over-indulgence or addiction to gadgets, alcohol, drugs, sex, gambling, food, rest, attention, praise and other desires. In such misery, you become a threat or burden to yourself, kids, family and the society.

Addictions are habits we gradually form over a long time till they become part of us. Like flood flushing all soils and objects blocking its flow, addictions flush away your capacity to resist impulsive desires. Though you may not have physical chains, addiction keeps you in bondage as a slave who has lost his will and cannot control himself. It is a habitual flow of energy to unhealthy purposes, which may not stop without redirecting the steady flow of energy to healthy purposes.[40] A major step in overcoming addiction is finding the positive purpose for stopping it, or

---

[39] Chukwunwike Enekwechi, "installing the behavioural antivirus in kids before they leave the factory - family" in *Restartnaija,* 26th February, 2019. https://restartnaija.com/2019/02/26/installing-behavioural-antivirus-kids/ retrieved 5th May, 2019.
[40] Restartnaija, episode 15 https://youtu.be/osW1zihm12s

identifying the perfection it denies you. For something good and tangible must grow or be growing to replace your addiction, otherwise it will reappear. The healthy purpose to redirect your energy is your social purpose, its revival, expansion or sustenance. So, instead of waiting to indulge or not indulge that addiction, you become proactive by consistently allocating the extra time or money for indulging the addiction to advancing your social purpose. There are practical ways for overcoming addictions at the end of this chapter.

"Attachment is the great fabricator of illusions; Reality can be attained only by someone who is detached." - Simone Weil.

<u>Modesty in displeasure</u> – displeasure is the uneasy feeling that comes from threat or event of losing something or experiencing pain. As humans, we naturally desire pleasure and are afraid of pain and lack of resources for pleasure and security. Yet, you cannot totally avoid pain if you wish to make positive impact and obtain true happiness. Nor can you obtain true happiness by dedicating your life to physical pleasure. Modesty in displeasure enables you choose the right amount of lack or pain as necessary sacrifice for your fulfilment. Your modesty manifests in the mode of response to displeasure:

- ***In human-inflicted pain or threat:*** when you are threatened, deprived or hurt by people, your first impulse is to retaliate in a most painful manner to subdue or kill the offender. The pain could come from people's military, manual, verbal or emotional attacks, social deprivation, or actions that affect your comfort, authority, honour or loved ones. If the offender is stronger or shielded, you bear grudge, waiting for the time to strike terror; or you transfer your frustrating anger on some innocent people or things. But if you are stronger, you retaliate directly with more pain, violence, war, murder or other forms of attack to get revenge and avoid appearing weak. Within or outside the law, retaliating with more pain satisfies your immediate desire for revenge and restores the fear people get when they think of offending you.

Yet, your response to offences or injustice depends on your priority to survive and satisfy your emotion, or to fulfil your purpose. If your priority is still a dream for growth and harmony, you redirect the revenge-energy to learn from the painful event in order to advance your purpose by modest, firm or honourable means. Then, handling offenders becomes correction *(sincere dialogue before force)*, instead of wasting productive energy on revenging every offence. And getting justice becomes retrieving your rights without losing your humanity. Voltaire insists that "we can only kill people who cannot be preserved without danger." When you eliminate or humiliate an enemy, you create two others from their relatives or sympathizers, and you set a precedence for your treatment. So, without focusing on growth and harmony, you destroy 'enemies' without considering its long-term effect on the people you wish to protect.

> *"You cannot bring back the ones you love; but you can honour their lives by helping others, it's the only way forward."*[41] *Your means to noble goals must be as noble as the goal you seek*
> – Martin Luther King Jnr.

- ***In circumstance-inflicted pain:*** life is filled with pains, which we always try to avoid and should avoid. Yet, whether you live to fulfil a social purpose or to survive in pleasure, you will still encounter pains from time to time. Understanding the difference between foolish pain and purposeful pain helps you use pain for fulfilment. Working, studying, discipline, mercy, lack, endurance, thinking, hunger, fatigue, sickness, accidents, bondage, loneliness and depression are classes of pain. If you choose surviving in pleasure, you keep running from all purposeful pains by cheating, robbing, lying or lazing around until foolish pain catches you as regret. But when your priority is fulfilling your social purpose, you evaluate and choose purposeful pains as sacrifices for developing and using your potentials for true happiness.

Virtue lies in the middle of your **approach** *to perfection to avoid extremism, not in your* **attainment** *of perfection, otherwise we embrace mediocrity as virtue.*
– Restartnaija

PROFESSIONAL TOOLS TO SOCIAL PURPOSE

Never ascribe to malice that which can adequately be explained by incompetence. –
Napoleon Bonaparte

Societies are organized so that people can actualize and utilize their various potentials for happiness through different professions. All professions in the society are individually directed to render services through any the three major pillars of social functionality: productivity, administration and security. Being in any of the three pillars allows you to steadily develop yourself, contribute to social growth and earn money, prestige and

---

[41] Jack Bauer to Chloe O'Brian, 24, season 9, episode 3

fulfilment. Though different professions are assigned to specific pillars of social functionality, they collaborate and support each other for common good. After observing the social organization for functionality, other people create other channels, known as entrepreneurship, for assisting the social structure and earning from the society.

The basic requirements for acceptance in these professions are talents, skills, qualifications and recommendations. But getting true happiness in professional establishments or entrepreneurial endeavours depends on some factors:

- **Efficiency:** Your talents and skills are tools for accomplishing results in the society, not just for making you feel good. The good you feel from your skills comes from the speed and accuracy of your results, not just the activities, pay, privileges and fame. If you have the talent, admit it and dedicate it to providing the results required in your professions especially against cynics.

- **Resilience and innovation:** Talent is like table salt, everyone has talent in one or more fields. What enables your talent to accomplish results is patient and consistent hard-work to use and improve them. Without innovating better methods you get stuck and possibly start blaming fate, bad-luck, enemies and other factors for your inability to improve and accomplish tasks.

- **Purpose:** True happiness in profession comes from enabling other peoples' productivity and social responsibility, not just getting money or power. Seeking only material happiness from your profession makes people jump from profession to profession in unhealthy competition. So, they cut corners, sabotage institutions and cheat for career raise or pay. But when internal happiness is your goal, you choose the profession that suits your social dream and resist foul plays even for covering your mistakes. And if the institution drifts from common good, or is not focused on social growth and harmony, you either initiate a reform or quit.

- **Physical fitness:** Taking care of your beauty, health, frame and look increases your confidence, acceptability and chances of success of impacting the world with your profession.

Despite your level of acquired or inherited comfort, acquiring necessary skills gives you more options to harmonize growth and attain fulfilment. With more skills, you allow other people focus on them as professions because they dedicate themselves to serve by it, not because you are incapable. Also, you don't become stranded during emergencies because you failed to acquire those skills.

MATERIAL TOOLS TO YOUR SOCIAL PURPOSE

Preaching against wealth in the name of religion, virtue or any philosophy is not only delusional, but deceptive. Despite your minds' powers and ideas, you need your physical body to actualize your social purpose; your body needs material wealth for health; and you need material wealth as tools to work and fulfil your dreams in the world. "Wealth consists in what is produced and consumed: food, clothes, houses, vehicles, factories, tools, schools, books, [gadgets] and churches..."[42] Wealth is not created by money, but by applying scientific knowledge on land and mineral resources to develop useful items.[43] Money is only a ticket people agree to use, or are forced to use, to represent and exchange wealth and services.[44] Without producing enough wealth from land and mineral resources, no amount of money circulation, ideas or skills can satisfy man's basic needs. So, poverty means lacking consistent products or services to exchange for other people's wealth. And a poor person is one who is not commercially productive, or whose productivity is not well-rewarded by the society or employer.

Land is the primary source and support for all wealth in the world. Some people inherit or purchase fertile lands, stable lands or lands that contain mineral resources for producing socially-relevant items. By owning such lands and resources, you can collaborate with other people to create wealth in the society. In creating wealth from those resources, you enrich the society by exchanging your products with other people's wealth. The productivity from your land motivates other people to increase their intellectual or material productivity so as to have products to exchange for yours. Also, using your productivity, you can encourage social responsibility by promoting ideas and producing items that enable responsible productivity.

Human instincts for territory make international organizations to support individual and group ownership of lands and property for production as human rights.[45] While some products can be easily used for fulfilment by increasing productivity and social responsibility, others are almost restricted for limited material happiness. For instance, using the

---

[42] Cf. Henry Hazlitt, *Economics in one lesson* (New York: Pocket books, Inc. 1946) p.149.
[43] Walter Rodney, op. cit. p.23.
[44] Chukwunwike Enekwechi, "Protecting Nigeria from foreign exchange manipulations" in *Restartnaija,* 10th December, 2018. *https://restartnaija.com/2018/12/10/protect-nigeria-exchange-rate/* retrieved, 25th May, 2019.
[45] Universal declaration of human rights, Article 17, number 2

time, resources or manpower enough for making hundred tractors to make two luxurious cars or yachts may not qualify as socially responsible productivity in a hunger-ravaged place. Whether under socialism or capitalism, such productivities are mainly enabled by governments that seize people's lands and mineral resources. In crony capitalism, capitalists influence local and/or foreign government policies to seize, privatize and exploit human (licensing) and natural resources for such productions.[46] In socialism, public officials violently seize and control people's natural and human resources for some discretionary and initiative-hindering equal distribution.

Where people are denied ownership of their lands and resources for material production, retrieving them becomes a primary goal. For without access to their resources for production, brilliant ideas for social responsibility die off without actualization. Then poverty, diseases, crimes and social decay obstructs your chance for true happiness through harmonized growth.

A sustainable millionaire is one who steadily produces or equitably contributes to producing goods or services that provide happiness for millions of people who have products to exchange for it. Not just supplying limited expensive luxuries to few social predators who impose and sustain unjust social structures for mass exploitation. Producing vital items for a people who are deprived of their resources for producing tradeable commodities bankrupts you, because they have nothing more to exchange for your products. Also, they become mentally dependent, greedy, unproductive and lacking chance for true happiness. Thus, despite having skills and products, you require a productive and trading population to complete your economic cycle of growth and harmony.

SOCIAL TOOLS TO SOCIAL PURPOSE

Social tool for life's purpose refers to your emotional connection in a social support system like family or close friends. These are people who have accepted you as their own based on blood links or other deeper links. They advise, encourage and support you in weakness and strength, as part of them, not just as a tool to exploit. These emotional links are important for fulfilling your social purpose, for no man is an island or programmed solitary robot. Despite getting new acquaintances on your ladder to social purpose, you do not abandon your social support system. And after all the bustling and hustling, you have someone or people to whom you belong, people before whom you can unwind, play, joke, laugh, drink, dance, cry, complain and feel human without all the formal scrutiny. Outright

---

[46] Cf. Dean Baker, *The conservative nanny state*, (Washington DC., Creative Commons, 2006), p.19.

loneliness is a killer that exposes people to vulnerabilities. And having people around simply because of what you have or the material things they can benefit from you is another level of loneliness.

DAILY SELF CONTROL

Consistent friction by the blade sharpens the sword
Repetition turns your actions and choices to character
'I fear not the man who has practiced 10,000 kicks once,
*But I fear the man who has practiced **ONE KICK 10,000** times"*
– Bruce Lee

So far in this book, we have discussed how to:

- Identify your target, which is the purpose of your life in and for the human society.
- Identify your bullets, which are the behavioural, professional, material and social tools for hitting your target.

Now we discuss how to sharpen these tools while maintaining focus on your target, despite changing routes, positions and distractions. You do not become an honest man because you spoke truth once, but because you speak truth always, even when it is hard. So, the most important virtue that supports all the others is courage. Without courage you cannot practice any other virtue regularly. Maya Angelou insists that "you can practice any virtue erratically, but nothing consistently without courage." Courage is the true requirement for freedom, since freedom is not the absence of constraints, but the courage and discipline to follow the rational rules we make for ourselves.

Don't get distracted – Keep your purpose daily in sight

Though you can choose alternative routes as plans b, c, d or e to your destination, you don't change your destination because of temporary difficulties on the current route. Also, many distractions to your life's purpose will disguise as great opportunities to gradually but certainly derail you. In competitions, battles and wars, distractions are effective ways of weakening an opponent's focus and capacity to win. So, few steps for focusing on your purpose include deciding and writing the following:

- ***Write down your purpose, its motto and image:*** the motto is a short statement that motivates or reminds you of your purpose and principles in various cases. Then choose a symbol or image that represents your goal or you on your way to your goal. It could be image of an animal, person, instrument, vehicle or any symbolic object that reminds you of your purpose.

- ***Qualities and skills you need to make the impact:*** this is not your regular academic training or certificate, but informal and social skills or behaviours you develop on your own. Learning a language, instrument, greeting, listening and conversation skills or other skills.

- ***Obstacles to your purpose:*** behavioural and competence obstacles like over-procrastination, lateness, fear, pessimism, shyness, isolation, laziness, addiction, body weight, ignorance, self-esteem, poor health, garrulousness or any other weakening feature.

- ***Choose one obstacle to conquer at a time or a quality/skill to acquire at a time:*** you cannot overcome all your obstacles or acquire all the skills/qualities at once. Instead, you list them and confront them one after the other by practicing the remedy over a long time. For instance, practising a language for 15 minutes daily for three months because you have to impact the speakers; choosing to perform an activity for only 5 minutes, instead of procrastinating. When you overcome one obstacle or target by steady practice, you choose the next on your list.

Develop your Daily Self-Control (DSC)

This is a list of activities you perform and regulate daily by marking [V], in order to cultivate desired habits for achieving your purpose. It incorporates activities for sharpening and applying your ideal, professional, material and social tools. Though you do not have much time, you create time for what you value. There are four sections of the daily self-control for managing your time.

DAILY SELF-CONTROL

Month: .... Year: ....

	1	2	3	4	5	6	7	8	9	10	11	12	13	14	15	16	17	18	19	20	21	22	23	24	25	26	27	28	29	30	31
P.E																															

Name: .... Witness: ....

Contact: .... Signature: .... Date: ....

Name: .... Witness: ....

Contact: .... Signature: .... Date: ....

- The **First section** *(2 lines for morning and afternoon reminders)* to hold your focus is your particular examination (PE). Here you write abbreviations for the practical step to confront the first obstacle you chose above, or first skill to acquire. The PE changes when you have cultivated the habit of excellence against the particular obstacle or acquired the skill.

- **In section** 2 *(the first 3 lines)* you evaluate your use of personal time and routine.

    ✓ In the first line, you mark [\/]to indicate you observed your morning routine which are:
    * Recalling and evaluating the dream you had the last night immediately after you wake up through meditation, yoga or prayer. You try fitting the dream in your reality, or leave it if it doesn't fit. Everybody dreams, some just ignore it, thereby forgetting and possibly missing clues to solving life's issues. Many answers and solutions came through dreams like Google from Larry Page, Elias Howe's sewing machine, James Watson's DNA method, Einstein's theory of relativity, Dimitri Mendeleev's periodic table, Niels Boher's atomic structure and many others. Ideas are forces of nature flying around to be captured and actualized by those who are attentive enough to identify and work on them. And if you don't remember the dream while meditating, just allow it be.
    * Do your quick indoor exercise, according to your state of life and health.
    * Arrange your room, bed or apartment. It takes less than 5 minutes. *The aim is not doing everything at once, but building habitual order around you from small exercises.*
    ✓ In the second line, you mark your social enlightenment efforts: Nelson Mandela says that "fools multiply when wise people keep quiet." Your role in social growth and harmony is not just judging mistakes, but correcting faulty social beliefs. You cannot know, evaluate or correct dominant beliefs without studying social indicators like music, movies, news and social media. When you identify and evaluate the dominant beliefs in the society, you develop and inject better beliefs and methods to true happiness. Even if you do not reveal your ideas instantly, daily jot them down for eventual disclosure as books, songs, movies, advice or posts to a wide or limited audience. In this way, you can educate the world for full happiness. You must not die with your ideas undisclosed.
    ✓ In the third line, you mark to indicate your night routine, which can

be: *Switch off gadgets (distractions), evaluate the day, check your day's events and mark your DSC.*

- **Section** 3 *(the second 3 lines)* guides your use of the basic ideals for your social purpose.
  - ✓ **Sincerity**: did I give true and enabling information to others [\ ], and did I fulfil my commitments to anybody I gave my word? [/] So the box looks like [\/] when you meet up in both enabling and action sincerity in a day.
  - ✓ **Generosity**: did I work to instantly or eventually provide palliative or liberating generosity to the environment or people without intention of publicity? The option for liberating generosity is similar to social enlightenment in the second line of the second section. Yet, you choose if you wish to add a palliative form of generosity in your list.
  - ✓ **Modesty**: Did I stick to my limits in engaging objects of pleasure and displeasure? In times of pleasure, did I stick to my set-limit or boundary in drinks, food, smoke, gadgets, games, intimacy, dance, fashion, speech or whatever? [\ ] In times of displeasure, did I control my emotions against excessive outbursts and uncalculated verbal or physical confrontation? [/] Uncontrolled anger, fear, sorrow or pleasure are weaknesses capable of draining your energy for reasoning, productivity and social responsibility.

- **Section** 4 (with four lines) guides your personal, professional, material and social tools.
  - ✓ Since humans are ever-becoming and rediscovering themselves by engaging the world, you engage the world daily. So, you mark: did I take time (minutes) to explore or engage my natural environment (and people) by playing, hunting, strolling, gardening or reading informal materials? Without playing, evolving and rediscovering yourself, your talents, passions, energies and environment, you become old and boring. Nature teaches, and "nature itself cannot err."[47]
  - ✓ Did I observe my dedicated time for career or academic growth? Even as an entrepreneur, you don't stop reading (even 15 minutes daily) to grow your knowledge in your field.
  - ✓ Did I observe my time for material production or investment? Even as service provider or intellectual, you can briefly study (even 10 minutes) to invest in material productions related to the service you provide.

---

[47] Thomas Hobbes, *Leviathan*, op. cit. p.37.

✓ Did I observe my dedicated time for social life (maintain relationship and have fun)?

Forming an effective DSC can take between two and four weeks of sincere self-evaluation, meditation and consultation. You must not begin all the sections at once. The self-evaluation helps you choose and regulate the sections that mostly apply to your state of life. Do not get confused when a chosen activity reappears in different sections, just mark it. Also, do not get discouraged or disappointed in yourself when there are many misses [.] on your DSC. Nobody is perfect. But by accepting your strengths and weaknesses, you consciously work on improving. Taking 5 minutes at the end of the day to check the Daily Self-Control can be difficult, especially when you think you are not improving as you expected. Yet the effect is worth the effort. If you miss marking the DSC on a night, you can mark it the next day. *Please find detachable copies of DSC before the back-page.*

Given six hours to chop down a tree I use the first
four hours to sharpen the axe - Abraham Lincoln
You cannot deeply impact the world without
ordering your personal life. — Restartnaija

<u>Formalize your purpose by having a witness:</u> you increase the seriousness of your marriage vows or other commitments by having legally competent witnesses. Likewise, you increase the commitment to your purpose by choosing a sincere witness to it. The highest reminder of your purpose is being accountable to someone to whom you give regular account on the progress. This is someone to whom you show your DSC, and discuss challenging areas. It may be a female or male clergy, mentor, sponsor, doctor, elder, friend, colleague, parent, sibling or lecturer. S/he does not have to be perfect, s/he just has to be sincere. Maintaining a witness for a long time is good for continuity. Yet, you choose to change a witness if you get uncomfortable with a witness or his/her questions.

Some people say "you cannot trust anybody". That is true. Yet, you cannot live a healthy life without trusting some people or institutions to some extent, even partially. Jorah Mormont responded to his Khaleesi "No one can survive in this world without help, no one." Without moderately trusting humans or institutions, you live in a hypersensitive siege mentality without friends, social life and influence. That is why you choose who and the aspects of your purpose you can disclose to your witness.

<u>Make it regular:</u> Joel Osteen insists that excellence is not a part-time job. You must be consistent in your developmental process, otherwise you keep crawling. Hence, you evaluate your progress or lapse with your witness at the end of the month, so you can objectively assess your growth.

> *Comfortable humans are like well-cleared and manured farmlands; if you are not directed to grow good fruits, you grow dangerous weeds. – Restartnaija. Thus, your freedom is not the absence of pain or limitation, but the discipline to set and follow your rules to fulfilment. – Jocko Willinks*

Chapter 5

FORMING OR JOINING THE RIGHT TEAM
Assemble and load the gun

Guns are powerful machines for confronting and subduing even the most ferocious beasts on earth. Different metal and non-metal parts like barrels, levers, springs, trigger, magazine or gunpowder work together in a gun. Without collaborating with other parts, none of the gun parts can perform the function of a fully assembled gun. Though it takes one person to make a difference, it requires more than one person for sustained social impact. Humans may be feeble and weak, yet you cannot achieve or sustain any social impact without collaborating with them.

You need other people to achieve your purpose
As bullets need guns to hit targets, you need human allies to achieve your social purpose and common good. Your social purpose alone cannot solve all the problems in the society or provide for everybody's fulfilment. A mason cannot complete a building alone without architects, labourers, electricians, plumbers, decorators and experts from other fields. You need other people for assistance, motivation, advice, moderation, continuity after your death or retirement and so on. There is no true social success without a successor to sustain it. Since compliance is not equal to commitment, you need committed people, not just compliant people or thoughtless followers.

With whom do you team up?
The initial instinct and most appropriate approach for getting collaborators is creating new groups to incorporate experts. Experts are trained and experienced people in their various fields, whose skills can easily initiate your purpose. Gathering experts just for their expertise may be difficult, expensive and shallow as their quest for profit and fame could override the

purpose. So, you can start from your existing informal groups by giving them a new purpose different from pursuing animal happiness. The existing informal groups you can incorporate for social purpose include:

- **The family**: Confucius insists that the strength of a nation derives from the integrity of the home. If the home is not stable and directed to social purpose, many people will miss the foundation for true happiness. This direction begins when you discover your life's purpose before marriage to choose someone to complement you.[48] Your spouse can either be a source of distraction or support to your purpose, not just a beautiful, handsome, famous or wealthy person. When you have a supporting spouse, both of you can guide your children to happiness by activating their responsible productivity. Even after marrying without finding your social purpose, you can still seek it and gradually direct your family to true happiness. Then your family can have a purpose, something to believe in, fight for and live for.

- **Religious groups:** Speaking about the emptiness of some religious piety, apostle James challenged, "Show me your faith without works, and I through my work will show you my faith." Moderate religious groups often focus on prayers, preaching, pity and almsgiving, while leaving active society-changing roles to the fanatic minority. Because of their lively proactivity, the minority fanatics gather more members and inflict immense havoc. The world is not just destroyed by the fanatic minority, but also by the moderate majority who failed to ***proactively infect*** others with active and responsible productivity. Instead of just preaching, prayer and almsgiving, educate people to extend their energies to productive social responsibility. And instead of just praying God to send good political leaders, you educate, inspire and sponsor good people to become leaders. For kindness and zeal without competence leads to doom.

- **Social groups:** Social clubs, professional teams, guilds, fans and old schoolmates often gather to eat, party, vacation or lobby without remarkable contribution to the society. Here, you can suggest an extension of the group's resources to contributing and enlightening the society for true happiness. Thus, Cicero notes that "friendship was given by nature to be an assistant to virtue, not a companion in vice."

---

[48] Chukwunwike Enekwechi, "Leading the family beyond financial security to fulfilment" op. cit.

- **Academic circles:** The specialisation and division of academic disciplines can distract you from the first purpose of education, which is common good.[49] It creates artificial divisions among people in the academia, and so, people get busy fighting for their discipline and profile, while the society suffers under divisive politics. Hence, apart from specializing in your disciplines, you could direct your energy to creating interdisciplinary structures that will enable harmonized growth through students, staff and teachers' unions.

Integrate your team to social purpose

Both lab scientists diagnosing a patient and prosecutors monitoring a suspect conduct investigations on their persons of interest. The difference between them is that while the lab scientist investigates you to heal you, the prosecutor investigates you to nail, jail or execute you. Despite your weakness, the medical team sees your potential for health and social contribution, and work to improve the health they see in you. But prosecutors see you as a suspect to be condemned and punished, or temporarily cleared and discharged without improving you. Being productive and socially responsible, you are like a medical practitioner working hopefully to improve people you meet, instead of just judging to bash them or briefly clap for them.[50] Redirecting your formal or informal groups to responsible productivity may take some gradual steps:

- **Be consistent with your social purpose:** The best way to teach is by example, especially yours. No matter your preaching and blaming, you cannot change anybody who has not decided to change. You can only be the reason why they decide to change, or the person guiding them when they decide to change. If they see you as a role model, they briefly follow you, until they find their own reasons to dedicate themselves or to give up.

- **Identify the good in them:** Despite signs of fear and evil in people "there is so much good in all of us, the best thing we can do is to help each other bring it out."[51] If you cannot see the good in people, you cannot positively influence, love or work with them.

---

[49] Chukwunwike Enekwechi, "Repositioning Nigerian education for productivity and progress" in *Restartnaija,* 21ˢᵗ April, 2018. https://restartnaija.com/2018/04/21/repositioning-nigerian-education/ retrieved 5ᵗʰ July 2019.

[50] Chukwunwike Enekwechi, "From social condemnation to social redemption: smartness vs greatness" in *Restartnaija,* 18ᵗʰ June, 2019. https://restartnaija.com/2019/06/18/from-society-condemnation-social-redemption/ retrieved 5ᵗʰ August, 2019.

[51] Game of thrones, season 6, episode 3, High Sparrow to King Tormen

Then, all you do is suspect, judge, condemn and avoid people in your smartness and self-righteousness.

- **Relate with the good you see in them:** Goethe insists that "If you treat an individual as he is, he will remain how he is. But if you treat him as if he were what he ought to be and could be, he will become what he ought to be and could be." After finding good qualities in the people around you, you relate with them according to their good qualities. For according to Abraham Maslow, 'what is necessary to change a person is to change his awareness of himself'.

- **Task and connect their energies to the society:** As footballers' efforts are aroused and held together in a team by hope of team-victory, people's energies are aroused and held together by hope of social progress. By showing how their individual roles contribute to social progress, they feel responsible for the society. Seeing results of their roles encourages them to do more. For humans derive true happiness by overcoming challenges, not hiding from challenges and appearing when others have overcome the challenges. Thus, after showing how their qualities can contribute to social progress, you assign them some suitable tasks. The task has to align with their specific qualities, for you do not reward a sheep's loyalty by giving it the function of a wolf. Their tasks could be in any of the following:

i. **Research for productivity or social responsibility:** Jiddu Krishnamurti states that "if we can really understand the problem, the answer will come out of it, because the answer is not separate from the problem." The first task is scientific research for productivity and social research for responsibility. This team interacts with the environment to discover its human and material potentials for productivity. Research is primary to any social change because "actions not backed by knowledge and knowledge not translatable into action, both cannot stand the test of time."[52] So, the research results guide the formation of social structures for harmonious growth.

ii. **Publicity/social education:** Erecting nice structures without educating the people for productivity and social responsibility is like designing beautiful parlours for pigs. They will sabotage what you have built. But educating people through videos, physical

---

[52] Pandurang S. Athavale

interactions, lectures or writings for productivity and social responsibility engages them for the society. Maria Montessori maintains that "establishing lasting peace is the work of education; all politics can do is keep us out of war." And Bill Gates states that "if you show people the problems and the solutions they will be moved to act." So, your group needs a team for simplified social education.

iii. **Advocacy team**: Despite its strength, a group needs partners, supporters, sponsors and funds to achieve harmonized social growth. Your goal is social progress, not just your personal or group's progress, or else you fall back to animal happiness. The advocacy team liaises with other bodies for synergy, and raises funds or social capital using their fame, skills and formal or informal links.

iv. **Implementation team:** After all the researching, some people will work to establish the ideal social structure for enabling productivity and social responsibility. This team engages the public, government and other bodies on policies and social functions.

- **Commend them:** Socrates says that social education is not like filling a vessel, it is lighting a flame, which continues burning on its own. Commending your associates for their efforts, even when the result is not perfect, inspires them to improve.

- **Give them DSC:** *"the fundamental strength of any enterprise lay in its people."*[53] Despite the size of its branches, a big tree that forgets its root source of nutrients will eventually collapse. Also, a group that forgets to fortify its members' individual integrity and training will crumble from within. For collective progress cannot override individual responsibility and personal growth. Hence, you inspire your group to use the DSC, and monthly collect the lower turn-out copy of the DSC as a sign of their commitment. Each person knows within him/herself how sincere s/he is with the DSC. For the worst person to deceive on earth is your own self.

'If you think in terms of a year, plant a seed; In terms of ten years, plant a tree; In terms of hundred years, teach the people.'
– Confucius

---

[53] Lee Kwan Yew, *From third world to first* (USA: HarperCollins, 2000), p.527.

Despite your readiness to involve people in your team, some people may at different times, have contrary intentions from social purpose. Some people are so invested in their fears and hatred, peace is the most threatening thing they can imagine.[54] They fear lowering their defence of material happiness in order to work with others for a better society. They fear lacking obvious edge, advantage or control over others. They fear responsibility, the unknown, missing their addictions and other forms of fear. You try to understand and rest their fears through education, while being careful against betrayal or selling out the group to highest bidders. Above all be sincere.

---

[54] Dalia Hassan, 24, season 8, episode 19, 10am – 11 am

Chapter 6

INSTITUTIONALIZE YOUR IMPACT

*"You are a political animal, even when hiding from politics;
if you want a social change, begin it yourself and introduce it
to the society. For until it becomes, or is supported by formal
policies, your impact stays hanging."* – Restartnaija

If a snake bites you, it deposits venom inside your bloodstream that destroys the systemic teamwork between your organs. While damaging the organs, the venom can be causing rashes on different parts of the skin. You cannot neutralize the venom or heal yourself by blaming the snake, blaming the yourself or covering the rashes with cosmetics. If you successfully mask some rashes on one part of the skin, other rashes will still appear on that part or other parts of your body. Instead, you treat the venom as the root cause of the rashes by identifying the type of snake to understand its viral load, and to develop and inject the appropriate antidote into the bloodstream to reset the venomous disorder.[55]

Likewise, you cannot heal your society just by blaming former colonialists, politicians or the desperate victims of social injustice. Nor can you succeed by focusing only on your profession or pretentiously ignoring the foreign and/or local root causes, which are restrictive beliefs that became laws, policies, institutions and traditions. You cannot curse-away,

---

[55] Adapted from Chukwunwike Enekwechi, "Entrepreneurship on a leaking foundation, e dey patch am, e dey leak" in *Restartnaija,* 7th August, 2018.
https://restartnaija.com/2018/08/07/entrepreneurship-e-dey-patch-e-dey-leak/ retrieved 30th June, 2019.

blame-away or pray-away institutionalized beliefs that hinder people from productivity and social responsibility. Instead, you ***educate*** people with enabling beliefs, and introduce them to the socio-political system. These are the people to reorder the social structure. They are the people to enable access to material and nonmaterial resources for productivity and social responsibility.

Some people insist that they hate politics. 'No, I don't like politics, it is dangerous, dirty, rough, wicked and foolish. I just want to stay in my world and live my life.' Yet, Plato insists that those who feel too smart to engage in politics are punished by being governed by those who are dumber. And, Bertolt Brecht maintains that:

> *"The worst illiterate is political illiterate; he hears nothing, sees nothing, and takes no part in political life. He doesn't seem to know that the cost of living, the price of beans, of flour, of rent, of medicine all depends on political decisions. He even prides himself in his political ignorance, sticks out his chest and says he hates politics. He doesn't know that from his political non-participation comes the prostitute, the abandoned child, the robber, and worst of all, corrupt officials, the lackeys of exploitative multinational corporations."*

Each society is a connection of persons, who are firstly members of families, villages, towns, clans and tribes, before states and country.[56][57] It grows from people's agreement to collaborate in developing and using their human and natural resources to satisfy their needs. To ensure peaceful collaboration, the people create laws and public offices to protect and guide the society on its purpose. Next, several members of the society strive to occupy and use these offices and laws to administer the society. The influences, intentions and competence of the people who occupy these positions determine their regime's impact on the society, whether progress or terror. Just like the moral education, intention and training of a man with gun influences what he does with the gun; protection or oppression. So, it becomes necessary to ensure that the positions are occupied by competent and responsible people, and that the laws are legitimately made for common good.

Law is a product of reason, made and promulgated for the common good by those who have legitimate charge of the community.[58] Unlike other definitions of law, this philosophical law-definition highlights the essence,

---

[56] Cf. Aristotle, Politics, Bk I.

[57] Cf. Thomas Hobbes, *Leviathan,* edited by Michael Oakeshott (New York: Macmillan Publishing Company, 1962) p.130-134.

[58] Cf. Thomas Aquinas, *Summa Theologiae,* Prima Secundae Pars, Q 90, A 4.

source, method and purpose of law. It emphasizes the primacy of legitimacy (free consent of the governed)[59] and common good in making laws. Other definitions present law as "a collection of rules imposed by authority,"[60] or "a rule of conduct imposed and enforced by the state", without stating the purpose and value of legitimacy. These latter definitions seem easily exploitable by smartly cruel people for suppressing others in many parts of the world.[61]

The people's productivity and social responsibility are the foundations of every society, while public administration and security are the pillars supporting the society. So, laws, which are instruments of public administration, are meant to direct the social relationship for people to discover, develop and utilize their potentials and resources for responsible productivity. Yet, law, which works by coercion, is not enough to get the best of people's collaboration. For individuals become more productive when they are educated and convinced about it.

'Food and drugs are important for human life; while food supports the bodies' growth, drugs poison[62] undesired growths in the body, then, supplements enable food to work properly. A person that eats right may not need drugs for a long time, but if he does not eat right, his body and immune system gets exposed to malignant growths – diseases. Plants, chemicals and other ingredients are used for producing both food and drugs, but in different processes and proportions. In the social order, the ingredients are different beliefs in a society; served foods are socially adopted beliefs, drug is criminal law and the supplement is civil law.[63] Without healthy beliefs, there may not be any law that can sustain peace and progress in a society. But where there is a high standard of morality (beliefs through proper education),[64] there is no need for law.'[65]

---

[59] Cf. United States Declaration of Independence,
https://en.wikipedia.org/wiki/United_States_Declaration_of_Independence
[60] "Law: Meaning, Nature and Characteristics" in *Kullabs*
https://www.kullabs.com/classes/subjects/units/lessons/notes/note-detail/6798 retrieved 16th February, 2018
[61] Chukwunwike Enekwechi, "Law as a tool of philosophy" in *Restartnaija,* 22nd February, 2018. https://restartnaija.com/2018/02/22/law-for-philosophy-legitimacy-and-common-good/ retrieved, 9th July, 2019.
[62] Anthony Ufere, *The good nurse* (Lagos: Sebana books, 2008).
[63] Criminal laws are laws whose violation leads to the penalties of government fine, jail or death. Civil law are used for resolving disputes, harmonizing people's relationships and extracting compensations for the offenses done by gross negligence, malicious intent or wilful disregard of other people's rights. http://www.differencebetween.com/difference-between-civil-law-and-criminal-law/
[64] Joseph Omoregbe, Ethics, (Lagos: Joja press, 2004). p7.
[65] Chukwunwike Enekwechi, "Law as a tool of philosophy" in *Restartnaija,* 22nd February, 2018. Op. cit.

Despite the primacy of education for productivity and social responsibility, law remains important to properly restrain or coerce uncooperative people to social order. Laws develop from prevalent beliefs in the society, whether restrictive or enabling beliefs, which are codified and passed down to younger generations. People inherit and often imbibe these beliefs, in form of laws and traditions without evaluating them in the light of true happiness. Thus, they can rigidly adopt expired or unhealthy beliefs as laws, which hinder them from fulfilling their social purpose in newer times. Even if the laws were initially made with good intentions, your political indifference allows an actively cruel or incompetent minority twist them. But, if you are actively involved, you will influence the law's development for harmonious growth, and can institutionalize your social purpose by attaching it to social laws. The process of adjusting society and its laws to support positive social purposes includes:

Evaluate the laws and process of social formation: Societies are governed by laws, which can obstruct or support the society's progress. Aspects of laws to evaluate for social progress are the origin, provision, enforcement and effect:

- **Origin (for legitimacy):** The first criterion for a law's capacity to yield harmonized growth is legitimacy. Legitimacy is the informed consent of the people governed by a law, which is freely obtained without imposition or coercion. A law or government becomes legitimate only if it comes from the "consent of the governed."[66] Yet, since it is difficult to steadily get individual consent from everybody in a society, a legitimate representation becomes necessary. Each person is firstly a member of a family and then community, a community that bonds with other communities to become state or country. And since humans are first, members of their families and communities before state or country, they legitimately agree or disagree with intercommunal or ethnic alliance, government and laws through their communities. When countries, governments and laws develop from different communities' agreement to collaborate for common good, your social purpose becomes easier through legislation. Integrating social purposes becomes like a freely consented marriage, where couples who have agreed to collaborate for harmonized growth adopt agreeable initiatives.

---

[66] Cf. Ayn Rand, *The Nature of Government,* https://campus.aynrand.org/works/1963/12/01/the-nature-of-government/page2

However, when communities are bound and held together without informed consent, the basic illegitimacy reduces the chances for harmonized growth. The relationship between the violently held communities becomes tensed and bitter like a forced polygamous marriage. In societies like this, institutions and laws are imposed through proxies, and endorsed by obstructionist-puppets who claim to represent various communities. And after some time, the disorganized people begin adjusting to the frustrating systems for survival. It worsens when younger generations grow into such situations without knowing the history of their obstacles. For this, George Orwell maintains that the most effective way to destroy people is to deny and obliterate their own understanding of their history. So, they behave like robots programmed by the historically imposed laws and social structures.

Thus, adjusting laws for social purpose demands historical evaluation of the law's origin for legitimacy. Though there may not be a perfectly legitimate law, the fundamental condition is that legitimacy grows from bottom to top or people to leaders, not from a brutal top to the suppressed bottom. This means that intercommunal alliances, governments, functions and laws derive from the individual's community representation.

- **Provisions (for belief):** Laws are products of beliefs meant for permitting and encouraging, or prohibiting and discouraging conducts in a society. Laws show the law-makers' beliefs about the people under the law in relation with their family, property, environment and other humans. It shows beliefs for valuing humans as objects to exploit for material happiness or collaborators to develop and engage for true happiness. Imposed laws, which lack historical legitimacy, usually provide avenues for exploiting people's rights to their human and natural resources. But legitimate laws, deriving from informed consent, makes provisions for people to develop their productivity and social responsibility. Provisions of a law show the lawmakers' view and preferred form of happiness.

- **Enforcement (for approach):** Who enforces the laws? How is it enforced? Despite the lawmakers' intentions, the efficiency of law for harmonized growth depends greatly on the enforcers. Their efficiency in executing the laws for harmonized growth depends on both their intellectual capacity and emotional attachment to the society. A person without emotional investment in a certain community may not value it, and a person with emotional attachment but lacking competence will destroy it with his incompetence. When a law-enforcement agent is drawn from one community and imposed on another community without considering communal loyalties, the result may not be positive. Law enforcement agents' competence and emotional investment in your target-place of social impact can support or impede your purpose.

The responsibility for deploying law-enforcement agents to specific locations depends on the provisions of the law. And with this provision comes the capacity to positively or negatively influence progress in the location. So, to secure the society for eventual progress, you evaluate the legal provisions for deploying law-enforcement agents in your place of social impact. This is to ascertain that the power to deploy law-enforcement agents is majorly dependent on the people within a community, who are emotionally invested in the community.

- **Short and long-term effects (for purpose):** law's major purpose is not immediate satisfaction of a few or conformity with tradition, but common good from enabling people's responsible productivity. So, if a law denies people resources for developing their capacities for productivity and social responsibility, it calls for abolition. "An unjust law is no law at all",[67] and people have a moral duty to oppose such laws.[68] Arguments about sustaining some laws end with observing the effects of the law in the society. Does it enable productivity, social responsibility and consequently, harmonious growth, or just satisfaction of a few at other people's detriment? If some people are arguing for some laws, but the social evidence shows mass insecurity, injustice, poverty, material unhappiness and internal emptiness, then their arguments are rendered useless by the social evidence.

Propagate relevant bills as pressure groups

After evaluating the laws, and the aspects that hinder harmonized growth, the next is to propagate bills to counter such provisions. These are the bills that create enabling environment for positive social purposes to flourish. They include bills to end institutionalized discriminations, exploitation, military suppression and deprivation of material and nonmaterial resources. Pressure groups educate people on their goals and diplomatic approaches to achieve them. The approaches include formal complaints through letters, reports and direct meetings with public officials before peaceful

---

[67] St. Augustine, Quoted In the memorial analysis of Martin Luther King Junior, in *An Unjust Law Is No Law At All: Excerpts from "Letter from a Birmingham Jail"* https://home.isi.org/unjust-law-no-law-all-excerpts-letter-birmingham-jail, January 20, 2014. Retrieved 19th February, 2018
[68] Cf. Joseph Omoregbe, *Ethics*, op. cit. p.6.

demonstrations, civil disobedience and finally, boycotting state activities. Without educating the public on the approach, your activities to remove hindrances to true happiness could be derailed to violence.

The highest check on tyranny in government is a people
who understand themselves and know what they want.
— Restartnaija

<u>Form political parties and sponsor advocates to leadership positions</u>
You would not need protests and demonstrations to get growth-enabling bills if the lawmakers have been educated for harmonized growth. They will simply incorporate supportive proposals to become laws for the society. When you have groups that are already devoted and connected for fulfilling social purposes, you can scale up such groups into a political party. Then, you can educate and sponsor good people among you to become leaders and lawmakers for a better society. This is because you cannot continue praying God to send you good leaders, when you can educate, motivate and sponsor good people to become leaders. When many competent and responsible people are in the social structure, they steer the society on noble principles. Stop expecting a political messiah. You are all your messiahs when you enlighten yourselves and collaborate for productivity and social responsibility.

After scaling up dedicated groups as political parties, the next step becomes working with people-oriented institutions. Winning elections or bills need tactical pacts with people-oriented institutions by pointing out chances for true, mutual and sustainable happiness with your collaboration. Humans are primarily linked to their local institutions like family, community, property and religion before more official national links. When the people are convinced of your competence and intention for achieving true happiness they will respond accordingly.

Despite your activism and individualized
interventions, your impact will remain unstable if
you do not connect it to the society's legal structure.
For public office is the highest position through which
you can connect your social impact, serve humanity
and bring the best out of your society. —
Restartnaija

Chapter 7

RESTART THE NATION

*"It is not enough to win a war; it is more important
to organize the peace"* – Aristotle

After defeating the Mad King, Robert Baratheon became king of Westeros. Before becoming king, he was a fierce military commander with keen eye for war. Despite his military strength and acumen, his reign was stained with bankruptcy and internal conflicts. Though he was excellent as a fighter and warrior, he was terrible and incompetent as a leader or administrator. His extravagant and reckless lifestyle plunged king's Landing into debts. Fighting and leading are different things, and they require different trainings and qualities. Likewise, winning elections, secessions or overthrowing dictators without knowledge, personality and will to organize people for responsible productivity is a tragedy. Your work does not stop at supporting candidates to overthrow tyrants or win elections. It extends to supporting them to achieve harmonized growth. Thus, Lord Varys defends the history of his political decisions and loyalties to the dragon queen, Daenerys Targaryen, saying:

"Incompetence should not be rewarded with blind loyalty. As long as I have my eyes I'll use them. I wasn't born into a great house. I came from nothing… I was sold as a slave and carved up as an offering. When I was a child, I lived in alleys, gutters, abandoned houses. You wish to know where my true loyalties lie? Not with any king, nor queen, but with the people. The people who suffer under despots and prosper under just rules. The people whose heart you aim to win. If you demand blind allegiance, I respect your wishes. Greyworm can behead me or your dragons can devour me."

We noted earlier that humans get true happiness by discovering and actualizing their potentials in the society.[69] And for this reason, people organize their societies to enable each person develop and use their potentials for the society. So, organizing, educating and enabling the people for maximum productivity and social responsibility is the major function of a government. And the ability to achieve this through regulations, policies and programs requires competence and dedication from both the leaders and citizens. Thus, even after electing good people to become leaders, you still need to check them against abuses both within and beyond national borders.

Despite the commonness of our humanity, which points to a common origin, it is difficult to accurately explain when and how humans spread so widely across tribes, nations, continents and races. Neither religious nor scientific explanations of human origin provides perfect answers on human dispersion across the world. Yet, the commonness of our humanity is undeniable, despite racial, religious, cultural or language differences. This feeling of sameness drives humans to collaborate for preserving life and humanity across national and continental borders. So, some people strive to improve the world and to make the world happier than they met it. But before making the world happier, you must organize your country and local terrain.

We owe duties to ourselves, to our nation and to the world,
duties that we do not accept grudgingly but gladly firm in the
knowledge that there is nothing so satisfying to the spirit than
giving our all to a difficult task. – Barack Obama

RESTART FOR NATIONAL MATERIAL HAPPINESS

In the earliest phases of human organization, production was scattered and atomized according to family and communal identity.[70] Each clan, community or kingdom produced what they needed from their resources, and later traded few of their products. Eventually, production advanced, leading to product specialization, larger industrial collaboration and socio-political alliances between former independent communities.[71] One community specialized in producing steel, another in rubber and another copper or leather, all to be used for manufacturing wagons. These industrial collaborations and socio-political alliances formed the basis of most

---

[69] Aristotle, Politics, Bk 1
[70] Walter Rodney, *How Europe underdeveloped Africa, 2009 edition* (Abuja: Panaf Publishers, 2009) p.217.
[71] Ibid. pp217, 139-140

industrialized countries and civilizations.

Thus, a progressive country is like a body with different interconnected parts working together for the whole body's sustenance. It consists of all lands, human, cultural and material resources contributing to the country's overall wellbeing. Like the human body, a country grows organically when all the parts are healthy and well connected to perform their functions. And as each part of the body requires other parts' assistance, each member requires other people's assistance to perform his function for the country. When some people are denied resources for developing and contributing their productivity and social responsibility, the country denies itself of those people's productivity and exposes itself to domestic threats. Using regulations and finance as loans, grants, shares or waivers, governments influence the growth or decline of productivity and social responsibility in various parts of a country.

A country has material happiness if its people have sufficient food, shelter, healthcare-insurance, jobs, security, comfort and physical pleasure. Even if all the citizens do not have sufficient provisions due to skewed policies,[72] majority have enough for mild sustenance. Willing and able-bodied people get jobs to support their families and loved ones from the society's productivity and social responsibility.

Industrial revolution began in Britain, in the 18th century, to change production process from using raw human energy to using steam-energy in powering machines. Afterwards, many industries sprung to increase productivity in mechanized agriculture, transportation, communication, construction and manufacturing. These new industries' high production capacities required more raw materials, some of which were sourced from underdeveloped societies. Further industrial revolutions, namely the second, third and fourth, birthed explosive wealth-creation and prosperity across the world. The increase from the different industrial revolutions responded to human desires for material happiness in the past two centuries. Most developed, high-earning or industrialized countries have attained high levels of material happiness and so, enjoy relative plenty. They attained such material happiness by adopting specialization principles and social structures for industrialization.[73] Aside random pains from mass shootings, loneliness, depression, suicide, racism and unchecked liberalism, the industrialized countries enjoy high levels of material happiness.

Despite the wealth-creation methods from the industrial revolutions, the underdeveloped countries still lack basic provisions for material happiness. People in such countries still live in lack of electricity, food, shelter, healthcare, security, scientific education and sustainable

---

[72] Cf. Dean Baker, *The conservative nanny state*, (Washington DC., Creative Commons, 2006), p.19.
[73] Francis E. Ogbimi, *Solution to mass unemployment in Nigeria* (Ile-Ife: OAU Press, 2007) p.41.

productivity. Mostly, the socio-political structures in such countries militarily restrict the people's access to resources for productivity and social responsibility. Most of the restrictive political structures came from historical conquests and continued foreign interference. ***"300 years ago, the British set out to occupy North America, Australia and New Zealand and to colonize much of Asia and Africa. They settled in the more desirable regions of Asia and Africa as conquerors and master."***[74] Despite the claim of independence, most of these societies, especially in Africa, still suffer effects of the imposed social disorder that basically restrict industrialization, productivity and social responsibility.

> *"Africa is given a reputation: poverty, disease, wars... These wars diminished in number after the turn of the millennium, but their chief cause - the lack of common nationhood — remains... Africa's nation states were formed by foreigners, lines drawn by Europeans on maps of places they had often never been to. They carved out territories, cut up kingdoms and societies of which they had little idea... they (African countries) lack a common conception of nationhood."*[75]

The structure for violently merging unconsented peoples as **'democracies'** and using rival neighbors to seize and exploit other peoples' lands and resources as international trade is the main deposit of colonialism.[76] With this hostile relationship between unconsented and historically disparate peoples violently bound up as democracies, there is no social foundation for productivity, loyalty or social responsibility. Thus, Lee Kwan Yew stated: *"I was not optimistic about Africa... I thought their tribal loyalties were stronger than their sense of common nationhood. Inter-ethnic peace, which had been enforced by the colonial overlord, was difficult to maintain after independence with power in the hands of an ethnic majority."*[77] The tribal and ethnic struggles for freedom and resource-control within the colonially-bound countries results in coups and countercoups, crisis, wars and dehumanization.

Now, those countries are like groups of people forcefully bound in a multi-cabin train with different passengers struggling to steer the train in a different direction, since there is no agreed destination. With the seizure and export of people's mineral resources, the principal industry in underdeveloped countries is now administration,[78] supported by religious

---

[74] Lee Kwan Yew, *From third world to first* (USA: HarperCollins, 2000), p.353.
[75] Richard Dowden, *Africa altered states, ordinary miracles.* (New York: Public Affairs, 2010), p.3.
[76] Walter Rodney, op. cit. pp. 277-278.
[77] Lee Kwan Yew, *op. cit.*, p.357.
[78] Walter Rodney, op. cit. pp.23.

and academic indoctrination.[79] So, politicians violently struggle to stay in power since there is almost no local productivity to sustain their acquired foreign tastes. To sustain foreign supplies, properties and luxuries they retain the colonial foundation for seizing and exporting the mineral resources people could have used for production. The effect of having a young and energetic population without access to resources for production is idleness and crime. The attendant poverty and hopelessness manifests in dehumanizing crises like mass-emigration, refugee-crises, human trafficking and awful deportations.

Restarting underdeveloped countries for material happiness requires socio-political adjustment based on the various people's human and environmental capacities for productivity. ***For underdeveloped peoples of the world to demand retribution for past wrongs was not the answer to survival.***[80] What develops a society is not the amount of imported products pumped in as retribution, aid or payment for cheap resources, but the people's productivity and social responsibility. Such productivity and social responsibility are not imported, commanded, looted or shared along ethnic and tribal lines.[81] Instead, they grow from cultural adjustments, socio-political reorganization, scientific education and industrialization. The political hype of sharing money for business while blocking the people's access to their mineral resources is like sprinkling water on seeds that were uprooted from soil and placed on concrete. None of them will take root or bear fruit, and the water (money) will quickly dry off from the sunny heat of over-taxation and import-dependency.

To get this socio-political reorganization for productivity, you require a sincere social research to distinguish the violently-bound peoples, including their lands and mineral resources. For there cannot be any sustainable peace without justice. The research outcomes will enable the people retrieve their lands and resources in order to discuss better partnership for human development, productivity and social responsibility. This distinction will compel practicable scientific education for the people to produce and trade what they need from their respective resources.

Having political power or benefitting from unjust socio-political structures can have hypnotic effects on its defenders. You may be reluctant to support a structural change, especially if you are benefitting personal animal happiness from the unjust social structures. However, there are momentary and historical prices for tyranny, its actors, supporters and

---

[79] Chukwunwike Enekwechi, "Education in Nigeria, liberation or indoctrination?" in *Restartnaija,* 23rd November, 2017. https://restartnaija.com/2017/11/23/education-liberation-indoctrination/ retrieved 27th August, 2019.

[80] Lee Kwan Yew, op. cit. 353.

[81] Chukwunwike Enekwechi, Transforming Nigeria's intertribal bitterness to neo-colonial liberation energy" in *Restartnaija,* 13th August, 2019. https://restartnaija.com/2019/08/13/transforming-nigeria-intertribal-bitterness/ retrieved 17th August, 2019.

beneficiaries. And whenever the spirit of humanity rises, humanity responds to strike social predators and tyrants, even from their children's hands who they have overfed with ideas of animal happiness.

> *It is no measure of health to be profoundly adjusted*
> *to a profoundly sick society.*
> – Jiddu Krishnamurti.

RESTART FOR NATIONAL FULFILMENT AND TRUE HAPPINESS

> *"For those nations like ours who enjoy relative plenty, we*
> *say we can no longer afford indifference to the sufferings*
> *outside our borders; nor can we consume the world's*
> *resources without regard to effect. For the world has*
> *changed."* – Barack Obama

We noted that true happiness comes from overcoming challenges to harmonized growth in the world. It does not come from hiding from challenges and reappearing for credits when others have overcome the challenge. Nor is it like material or animal happiness we derive from satisfying physical desires of narrow pleasure and security, even at other people's expense. True happiness is the product of inner greatness, the only quality that can sustain growth, peace and security in the modern world. Thus, countries with true happiness are great countries where people are maximally productive and feel socially responsible, not just for themselves, their families and countries, but for the world. This productivity and universal responsibility manifests in their political structures, social orders, domestic and foreign policies, institutions and laws.

Some international policies, alliances, interests, power-plays and class struggles have been established for universal social responsibility. One of such treaties was the Cross-Atlantic charter that laid foundations to end direct colonialism and foster global political independence.[82] Other political alliances have been forces of global development and leadership in the recent years. Their drive for growth and harmony enabled researches that brought several inventions, breakthroughs and interventions. The abolition of slave-trade in respect for the sanctity of human life and replacement of gladiators with skilful footballers and sportsmen also rose from such

---

[82] Oladele Fadeiye, *Essays on modern world history,* (Lagos: Murfat publications, 2009), p.190.

alliances. More of such treaties involve mediation agents, efforts and institutions for human rights, globalization, economy, finance, trade, geopolitics, terrorism, crime, security, climate, ecology and environment, sustainable development, nation and state sovereignty, diplomacy and relations[83] between peoples, groups, countries, regions and organizations.

Challenges to restarting for national true happiness

The awful condition of many underdeveloped countries after these scientific, military and economic interventions raise questions about their sincerity. Were they done through deception and coercion for exploiting the structurally-subdued parts of the world? Were they truly intended for world growth and harmony, or for formalizing exploitation channels like hyenas holding and eating a live animal's internal organs while decorating its head? Despite claims of spreading development, a pattern of underdevelopment appears under these interventions as follows:

- **Endorsement of large-scale political captivity as democracy:** one of the greatest writers, Aeschylus, noted that *"in every war truth is the first casualty"*. The prosperity that followed America's freedom-drive at independence shows the necessity of modest freedom for human development. Without the political freedom to own, develop and use their human and natural resources, humans may never develop nor actualize their potentials. This political freedom flows from people's consent to be governed by their chosen system of government. This is the right to self-determination, allegedly assured by United Nations. However, the international reference to brutal and colonially-forged constitutions and countries of unconsented peoples, as democracies, remains the foundational lie for neo-colonial exploitation.[84] For he who cast the foundation of a building has indirectly set the limit for its growth.

  Currently, many unconsented African and Asian tribes, groups and nations typify political captives, militarily held under mock-countries. And the imposition of 'Western Democracy', Structural Adjustment Programs, rebel-militarization and regime-changes become international tools for social disorganization. Also, the international endorsement of flawed elections and the indifference to calls for referendums become suspect. Without reorganizing the unjust social foundations and legal conditions, the cycle of tyranny

---

[83] Paul McDaniel, "What is international politics?" in *Classroom,* September 29, 2017. https://classroom.synonym.com/what-is-international-relations-12079692.html/ retrieved 20th June, 2019

[84] Chukwunwike Enekwechi, "Is the truth always bitter?" op. cit.

continues since "cruel leaders are made only to have new leaders turn cruel."[85] Imposing legal systems for political prisoners to periodically elect their prison warder is not democracy,[86] but rotational dictatorship. Such 'death-race' political structures can only produce different variations of Frankenstein. And people keep fighting to become favourite slaves to former colonialists.

- **Exploitation of captive's resources as international trade:** A man who knowingly buys stolen goods indicts himself as an accomplice to robbery. Endorsing large-scale political captivity is not an end in itself. It provides avenues for foreign interests to use rival neighbours to hold and exploit people who would not have allowed such direct exploitation. The main reason for colonialism was to exploit resources for European industries, often using neighbouring dictators.[87] Before leaving at independence, these rival neighbours were forcefully merged as countries under colonially-made constitutions to enable indirect exploitation. With such fake foundations, postcolonial administrators get foreign military and logistic support to exploit and trade people's resources for consolatory finished products.[88][89] Later, the foreign assistants provide safe havens for corrupt officials to store looted funds from the consolatory revenues.

- **Fostering dependence by intellectual protectionism and palliative aids:** Teach a man to fish and he becomes self-sustaining; but deny him the knowledge while giving him fish and he will depend on you forever. Endorsing large-scale political captivity for exploitation also requires mentally discouraging the people from attempting to use mineral resources for productivity. Thus, some foreign scholars and experts claim that people in underdeveloped countries lack intellectual capacity to understand modern industrialization. Recounting how British experts claimed in the 1960s, that it would take the black man 500 years to understand the dynamics of modern productivity, Chinua Achebe wrote: ***"We were told that technologically we would have to rely for a long, long time on the British and the West for***

---

[85] Che Guevara, www.brainyquotes.com

[86] Chukwunwike Enekwechi, "Our leaders for where, our brotherly jailers they are" in *Restartnaija,* 28th October, 2017. https://restartnaija.com/2017/10/28/our-leaders-our-brotherly-jailers/ retrieved 27th August, 2019.

[87] Walter Rodney, op. cit. pp.277-278, 317.

[88] Cf. Mogobe Ramose, "Discourses on Africa" in *The African Philosophy Reader, Second Edition,* Edited by P. H. Coetzee and A. P. J. Roux (New York: Routledge, 2003). p.3.

[89] Walter Rodney, 293-295.

everything."[90] The claims were quickly refuted as the defunct Biafra's Research and Development team refined petrol and produced communication gadgets, bombs and arms within two years of the colonially-backed civil war.[91][92]

But after the war, these technological advances were suppressed to sustain unproductivity in the exploited societies.[93] Since then, academic advances in the underdeveloped societies lack practical steps to original, resource-based productivity. *"In the colonial society, education is such that it serves the colonialist… In a regime of slavery, education was but one institution for forming slaves."*[94] Apart from tactically frustrating industrial efforts in underdeveloped places, international media and aid-agencies portray them as perpetually helpless. Relating to the hypocrisy of postcolonial interventions, British journalist, Richard Dowden, recounts:

> *"The aid workers tell the journalists where the disaster is breaking. The aid agencies provide plane tickets, a place to stay, vehicles, a driver, maybe a translator - and a story. In return the journalists give the aid agencies publicity, describing how they are saving Africans and using images of distress and helplessness to raise money. This deal excludes the efforts of the local people to save themselves. It is easier and more lucrative to portray them as victims dependent on western charity."*[95]

Instead of supporting industrial efforts for productivity, foreign interest-agents recruit few natives to market their finished goods as entrepreneurs, explore business opportunities as researchers and advertise palliative generosity as brand ambassadors, fellows or messiahs. Hence, the SDGs' efforts to liberate underdeveloped countries may never yield fruit without addressing the social foundations of unproductivity. And many people in the underdeveloped countries are getting convinced that "no European nation is ready to genuinely support the aspirations of African [and other underdeveloped] countries for smooth industrial take off."[96]

---

[90] Chinua Achebe, *There was a country* (USA: Penguin books, 2012), p.157.

[91] Joshua Akinwumi, "I nearly ran mad when my mother died few days after I travelled to England" in *Punch,* 21, July 2018. https://punchng.com/i-nearly-ran-mad-when-my-mother-died-few-days-after-i-travelled-to-england-akinwumi/

[92] Chinua Achebe, *op. cit.* p.157.

[93] Joshua Akinwumi, op. cit.

[94] FRELIMO (Mozambique Liberation Front) Department of Education and Culture 1968, quoted in Walter Rodney, op. cit. p.246.

[95] Richard Dowden, op. Cit. p7

[96] Oladele Fadeiye, *European conquest and African resistance* (Lagos: Murfat publications, 2011) p.165.

- **Economic bondage through loans:** The person who feeds you controls you. The outcome of frustrating industrialization in underdeveloped countries is increased unproductivity, scarcity and demand for finished products. This increased demand raises the pressure on foreign products and the cost (quantity of crude resources required) for fewer consumer products. Thus, underdeveloped countries supply more or pledge future resources at cheaper prices as loans for fewer consumer products.[97] This is why underdeveloped countries remain poor, weak and always indebted to the industrial-protectionist countries and multinationals. While escaping from Thai insurgents in the movie "No escape",[98] British agent, Hamming, explains to American engineer, Jack Dwyer, how developed nations use international relations, foreign interests and policies to exploit underdeveloped countries:

"I am the one who started this shit. Guys like me pave the way for guys like you to wind up here. They [locals] don't usually fight back, most of the time they don't even realize what we are doing. We have interest in this region [Thai]. Our countries, the corporations who run them have interests here. So I show up all nice and friendly offering to get them a loan to pay for our services, which we know they can't afford. Then we build them power-plants, waterworks, freeways, it doesn't really matter. And when they can't repay us, then we own them. The rebel leaders say that we are trying to enslave their people by controlling the waterworks. They were right. Most of those merciless men out there, they are just trying to protect their children just like you."

<u>Steps in restarting for true national happiness</u>

Restarting your country for true happiness, as different from animal happiness, implies evaluating and adjusting domestic and foreign policies, treaties and alliances frustrating harmonious growth in other parts of the world. It includes forming treaties that enable global productivity and social responsibility for harmonious growth. Stating the effect of nationally seeking animal happiness over true happiness, Vladimir Lenin asks: "Can a nation be free if it oppresses other nations? It cannot." So, you may not be excused by the patriotism-tag for being indifferent or enjoying animal

---

[97] Chukwunwike Enekwechi, "Protecting Nigeria from foreign exchange manipulations" in *Restartnaija,* 10th December, 2018. Op. cit.
[98] Mitchell Litvak, David Lancaster, Drew Dowdle, "No escape", 2015.

happiness at other people's expense.

Patriotism is often applauded as a most noble disposition, and many people are celebrated for being patriotic. Yet, President David Palmer advised Agent Aaron Pierce about his son's military ambition: "It's a fine thing to defend one's country, but make sure the cause he is fighting for is the just cause."[99] So, despite the national applause, each individual owes him/herself a humane justification for actions taken as patriotism or **'following orders'**. For, government approval of tasks as patriotic duties on morally-independent people does not remove the people's responsibility or guilt. And governments' adoption of laws or treaties is not enough justification for citizens, intellectuals and military to accept or defend them without thinking.[100] Many conscientious citizens protest against unnecessary invasions, wars or inhuman activities in both foreign and local territories. Some join aid or missionary works in affected areas as reparations for damages done in their name,[101] or kind contribution to harmonized growth. However, addressing the issue more officially and lastingly would require more socio-political steps like:

- **Support social reform for responsible productivity in the colonially disorganized and underdeveloped societies:** As noted earlier, a society is like a car or body with various parts working together for proper functionality. And the measure for a society's functionality is its productivity and social responsibility. So, if a society has never been industrially productive, like a car that has never moved on its own, the basic remedy is to reorganize the structure. This means dissecting the socialistically conjoined peoples and their resources, for them to discuss and agree on partnership modes for productivity and social responsibility. Such reordering inspires individual and group productivity before advanced social alliance and industrial collaboration. This is better than pumping in loans and aids that quickly return to industrialized nations as payment for consumer products and non-regenerating assets – flashy infrastructure.

  "NGOs, World Bank, United Nations have little interest in understanding African difference, how it works. But aid agencies, western celebrities, rock stars and politicians cannot save Africa. Only Africans can develop Africa. Outsiders can help but only if

---

[99] 24, season 2, episode 22

[100] Chukwunwike Enekwechi, "From human to patriot, more emotional than mechanical", op. cit.

[101] Martin Pengelly, "Georgetown students vote to pay reparations for slaves sold by university" in *The Guardian*, 15th April, 2019. www.theguardian.com/world/2019/apr/15/georgetown-students-reparations-vote-slaves-sold-by-university. Retrieved 15th August, 2019.

they understand it, work with it."[102] "Many American leaders believed that racial, religious and linguistic hatreds, rivalries, hostilities and feuds down the millennia could be solved if sufficient resources were expended on them…[103] However, it was not true that all it needed to fix a problem was to bring resources to bear on it."[104]

Violently taking, merging or selling people's resources for socialist 'equality' in distribution or income is the highest producer of injustice,[105] corruption[106] and poverty in the world. It opposes the basic principle of growth, which is freedom. It cannot inspire growth. Instead, it inspires laziness, greed and cowardice to impoverish the world by rewarding unproductivity. Free healthcare, free education, free infrastructure and free amenities are not free; they come from people's exploited labour, seized resources or given to you as indirect loans. Loans you *must* pay back or forward to the person, family, relative or society that made it possible.[107] So, you must retrieve your resources,[108] proudly produce something and contribute to the cycle of life and growth, instead of waiting for government welfare or handouts.

Once people are free to discover, develop and use their potentials and rightful resources to solve problems, earn income, dignity and happiness, forcefully equating people's income is injustice. If you are not ready to look inwards to find and develop your potentials and resources for a productive and dignified life, no responsible government, institution or person on earth can sustain you. Yet, the society remains responsible for exceptional cases where few people truly require charity for development due to disability or misfortune.

Without reorganizing their societies for productivity, people from underdeveloped countries will continue trooping in and terrorizing the developed countries with crimes. And despite your academic defences, you will not have a true moral justification for deporting them while

---

[102] Richard Dowden, op. Cit. p7.

[103] Lee Kwan Yew, op. cit. p 451.

[104] Lee Kwan Yew, op. cit. p. 451.

[105] Chukwunwike Enekwechi, "Africa's mixed economy: freedom without responsibility" in *Restartnaija,* 27th November, 2018. https://restartnaija.com/2018/11/27/africas-mixed-economy-irresponsible-freedom/ retrieved 4th August, 2019

[106] Chukwunwike Enekwechi, "Fighting corruption in Nigeria with the wrong tool" in *Restartnaija,* 12th September, 2017. https://restartnaija.com/2017/09/12/fighting-corruption-in-nigeria-wrong-tool/ retrieved 4th August, 2019.

[107] Chukwunwike Enekwechi, "The necessary pride for Nigeria's redemption" in *Restartnaija,* 27th August, 2019. https://restartnaija.com/2019/08/27/necessary-pride-nigeria-redemption. Retrieved 30th August, 2019.

[108] Chukwunwike Enekwechi, "Organizing the true national conference for a new Nigeria" in *Restartnaija,* 5th February, 2019. https://restartnaija.com/2019/02/05/organizing-nigerian-national-conference/ retrieved 4th August, 2019.

contributing to their woes through the baptized robbery called international free trade. There cannot be sustainable peace and development without justice, instead suppression rules.

- **Trade or negotiate resources with original owners:** Like drugs, arms or human trafficking, as long as there is free market for stolen resources, international vampirism will not stop. And as long as international players and World Trade Organization retain the baptismal name for indirect exploitation as free trade, it will only increase. A clear confirmation for supporting individual and communities' freedom for responsible productivity will be recognizing their ownership of their resources. This recognition provides foundation for treaties to criminalize the invasion, exploitation and trade of people's resources by others, especially colonially-enabled dictators. So, mineral resource dealers will be required to negotiate directly with individual or communal resource owners, who will eventually pay appropriate taxes.

  Developed nations who have been benefitting from postcolonial exploitation as international trade may fear such treaties. Their concerns will be: ***"how do we sustain our luxurious lifestyle if cheap resources stop flowing from underdeveloped countries?"*** Spoilt children become greedy and wasteful from easily getting surplus provisions without toiling for them. Also, most wasteful societies directly or indirectly exploit underdeveloped countries for increased animal happiness. They include those who spend lots of time, human and material resources on cosmetic drugs and extreme liberalism,[109] when the exploited people only need few of those resources for life-saving medication, food and education. They spill and neglect some of these resources as waste or pollution, while exploiting preferred resources from underdeveloped countries. Yet, "pollution is nothing but the resources we are not harnessing."[110]

  As part of restarting your country for true happiness, you push bills for negotiating and trading with the rightful resource-owners. Second, you adopt national prudence in using resources, and start researching on better usage for the resources neglected as pollution or waste. Third, you educate your society for prudent productivity from available resources, instead of promising them more animal happiness from baptized international robbery.

---

[109] Cf. Chukwunwike Enekwechi, "Managing the danger of freedom in a modern and complex world" in *Restartnaija*, 6th November, 2018. https://restartnaija.com/2018/11/06/managing-freedom-complex-world/ retrieved 30th July, 2019.
[110] R. Buckminster Fuller.

Great leaders are not like *'Santa Claus'* sharing free gifts. Instead, they are like midwives who enlighten and enable people to bring out the best in them.[111] Thus, Thomas Jefferson says: "If a nation expects to be ignorant and free, in a state of civilization, it expects what never was and never will be." Theodore Roosevelt also warned his countrymen about the consequence of focusing on animal happiness by stating that "the things that will destroy America are prosperity at any price, peace at any price, safety instead of duty first and love of soft living and the get-rich-quick theory of life." Hence, you must educate your people to seek true happiness from their highest degree of productivity and social responsibility.

> *"All life demands struggle. Those who have everything given to them become lazy, selfish and insensitive to the real values of life. The very striving and hard work that we so constantly try to avoid is the major building block in the person we are today."* – Pope Paul VI

- **Intellectual liberalism for productivity and social responsibility:** The claim that some races are intellectually inferior or superior remains false. And using these claims as excuses to hide fundamental industrial ideas even after recouping invested profits amounts to self-deception. No scientific discovery or knowledge is obtained in national or group isolation, or totally free of other people's contributions and influences. Maria Currie insists that "science is essentially international, and it is only through lack of the historical sense that national qualities have been attributed to it." Noting his experience at the American citadel of knowledge, Lee Kwan Yew recounts:

> *"Harvard was determinedly liberal. No scholar was prepared to say or admit that there were any inherent differences between races or cultures or religions. They held that human beings were equal and a society only needed correct economic policies and institutions of government to succeed."*[112]

To harmonize growth for true happiness, you support treaties for

---

[111] Chukwunwike Enekwechi, "The midwife leader: the leader Nigeria needs" in *Restartnaija,* 23rd March, 2018. https://restartnaija.com/2019/02/23/midwife-leader-leader-nigeria-needs/ retrieved 30th August, 2019.

[112] Lee Kwan Yew, From third world to first (United States of America: Harper Collins, 2000), p 461

intellectual liberalism for increased global productivity and social responsibility. This liberalism does not imply freedom for reckless experiments that coerce, exploit or endanger humans and threatened animals or plant species.[113] Nor does it imply a careless declassification of delicate information that can threaten people's identity or security. Instead, it implies openness to productive data-sharing, effective transfer of scientific knowledge and apt research disclosures for enriching humanity. It also involves establishing the type of foreign direct investments that can develop people's technical knowledge and resource-based productivity.[114] This contributes more to national true happiness than coldly exploiting deprived people for animal happiness through resource exploitation firms, shallow investments and speedy capital repatriation.

- **Enlightened partnership over domineering relationship:** Seeking national true happiness requires courage. First, courage to accept past, present and possible truths about our common humanity, and second, courage to adjust to these truths. Most debts holding underdeveloped countries below developed countries are incurred from importing and installing depreciating and consumer goods and services.[115] Proper social reorganisation, direct trade with resource-owners and intellectual liberalism will reduce underdeveloped countries' dependence toward a dignified partnership between nations. Yet, some developed countries benefitting materially from the status quo will wish to frustrate possibilities of level partnership. This is because they are either benefitting from brain-drain and resource-leakage in disorganized societies, or from a delusional sense of superiority or pride in seeing that there are people lower than they are. This is the delusion of being higher humans than others, which leads to animalistic struggle for positions and resources as justification of racial superiority. Eventually, by understanding the need for national true happiness, they will accept a world of enlightened partnership and experience national fulfilment.

After liberating Tyrion Lannister from King's Landing, Lord Varys hinted

---

[113] Tom Beauchamp and James Childress, *Principles of biomedical ethics*, 5th edition (London: Oxford university press, 2001).

[114] Cf. Lee Kwan Yew, *From third world to first,* (United States of America: Harper Collins, 2000), p.53-55.

[115] Cf. Mogobe Ramose, "Discourses on Africa" in *The African Philosophy Reader, Second Edition,* Edited by P. H. Coetzee and A. P. J. Roux (New York: Routledge, 2003). p.3.

on the possibility of a just world.[116]

>**Varys:** I want peace, prosperity, a land where the powerful does not prey on the powerless.
>**Tyrion:** The powerful has always preyed on the powerless, that's how they become powerful in the first place.
>**Varys:** Perhaps we've grown so used to horror, we assume there's no other way.[117]

Competitions are crucial for development when they are healthy and directed to socially responsible productivity; not when they are used to suggest people's racial or inborn superiority through positions and acquisitions. Despite the cultural rivalry between the left and right hands, they need each other to balance the body movement and perform various activities. Without amputation, the right hand cannot climb a mountain leaving the left hand tied to the ground beneath a cave.[118] Trying to amputate or weaken one hand to favour the other leads to a major deformation of the whole body. Also since humanity is one, you cannot dehumanize anybody without first dehumanizing and deforming yourself morally, rationally[119] or physically. Without guiding human energy to productivity and social responsibility, humans will be destroyed by their own fear and greed.[120] The link in humanity is that we are all humans, the beauty is that we have the rational instinct for social responsibility, the limit is that we do not know everything, the power is that we can develop a lot when we collaborate and the message is that we do not become stronger by making other people weaker.

"We cannot build our happiness on the unhappiness of someone else. Some people could, but not people with a burden of conscience."[121]

---

[116] Game of Thrones, Season 5, Episode 1 by David Benioff and D. B Weiss
[117] Game of Thrones, Season 5, Episode 1 by David Benioff and D. B Weiss
[118] Chukwunwike Enekwechi, "racism and the spirit of sportsmanship" in *Restartnaija,* 29th May, 2018. https://restartnaija.com/2018/05/29/racial-rivalry-sportsmanship/ retrieved 5th August, 2019.
[119] Mogobe Ramose, op. cit. p.3-4.
[120] Chukwunwike Enekwechi, "Has the West become the demon of the world?" in *Restartnaija,* 3rd February, 2018. https://restartnaija.com/2018/02/03/has-the-west-become-demon-of-the-world/. Retrieved 5th August 2019.
[121] Richard to Kay, the movie "Married life" directed by Ira Sachs, 2007.

CONCLUSION

*A perfection of means and confusion of **aims**, seems to be our main problem.*
Albert Einstein

All elements actualize their potentials by performing specific functions that nature assigns to them for sustaining life on earth. Plants and animals have specialized structures like shoots, wings, paws, horns, claws, teeth, horns that define their growth process, survival, adaptations and activities. But man is born without specialization, and so, has to discover his purpose and the potentials for actualizing them. With his natural gifts of reasoning, creativity and transcendence, man discovers his purpose, as well as the potentials and resources for fulfilling his purpose. Without finding his purpose and developing the potentials and resources for fulfilling his purpose in the rightful place, he will be floating around like a ship on the sea without destination.

This book is written to show man's position as the centre and prime of nature, and how he can advance from developing himself as an individual to enabling harmonized progress in the world.

> *"Discipline changes animal nature into human nature. Animals are by their instinct all that they ever can be; some other reason has provided everything for them at the outset. But man needs a reason of his own... he has to work out a plan of conduct for himself."[122]*

In chapter one, we identified happiness as man's goal in life, and distinguished between material or animal happiness and internal happiness or fulfilment. Material happiness is the good feeling you get by getting and using resources mainly for yourself, while internal happiness is the inward

---

[122].Immanuel Kant, *Education,* translated by Annette Churton, (USA. University of Michigan press, 1966), p.2.

satisfaction from getting and using resources for growth and harmony in the world. Also, we identified reasoning, creativity and transcendence as nature's gifts for man to use natural resources and forces to support growth and harmony in the world. If man does not understand his central role as manager in nature, he begins 'living to have', which means acquiring resources only for his material happiness. But when he understands his managerial role in nature, he begins 'having to live', which means acquiring resources for supporting growth and harmony in the world.

In chapter two, we evaluated the people who benefit from our decision of 'having to live'. Before identifying who deserves to benefit from us, we clarified that people can verifiably benefit only from our material and nonmaterial productivity. So, if we do not have material or nonmaterial productivity, we may not claim to be living for anything. After evaluating the choice of living for God through religions, living for our family alone and living for our country, we observed that none of them assures us of true happiness. Hence, we chose living for humanity and working for common good.

In chapter three, we discussed the act of redefining your purpose by discovering your social dreams, your talents and dispositions, and then, your location of influence. Discovering these three elements gives you a focus for living a meaningful life. We noted that your purpose is not your career, profile, awards and certifications, but the impact you make in supporting growth and harmony in the world.

In chapter four, we discussed the process of developing the tools for fulfilling your purpose. These tools include the behavioural ideals of sincerity, generosity and modesty; the professional tools of efficiency, resilience, purpose, physical beauty and fitness; material tools which are natural resources and physical products, and then social tools which are the relationships you build with people around. After, we showed how to set up Daily Self-Control (DSC) for turning these tools to habit through repetition.

In chapter five, we discussed how to form the right team with whom you can contribute to social growth and harmony. We noted that you must not form an official team of experts, but can begin by giving a new purpose to your informal groups like family, religious, social and academic groups. You integrate them for social growth and harmony by being consistent in your social purpose, identifying and relating with the good in them, directing their energies to relevant sections, commending them and introducing them to DSC.

In chapter six, we discussed the process of scaling up your efforts to harmonize social growth by linking it to the social structure. We noted that without linking your social efforts to the social structure, it will continue hanging in the air without roots. The steps include evaluating your national laws and their process of formation; propagating relevant bills as/using pressure groups; and forming political parties to educate and sponsor good people to leadership positions.

In chapter seven, we discussed the process of restarting your nation for national material happiness, and then for national true happiness. The task of restarting the nation for material happiness is mainly for underdeveloped countries, whose citizens are structurally disorganized and deprived of material and nonmaterial resources for productivity. Their task is to reorganize their social structure for people to individually or communally own and manage their resources for productivity and social responsibility.

The task of restarting the nation for national fulfilment or true happiness is mainly for industrialized nations, who truly wish to contribute to global growth and harmony. Many of such nations have made international policies, treaties and interventions that portray their eagerness to contribute to global growth and harmony. However, these efforts seem ineffective owing to some challenges that include endorsement of large-scale political captivity as democracy, exploitation of victim's resources as international trade, fostering dependence by intellectual protectionism and palliative aids, and sustaining economic bondage through loans.

Truly restarting their nations for national fulfilment or true happiness will require ending some treaties that obstruct other people's productivity and social responsibility, and forming new treaties to enable global productivity and social responsibility. These involve treaties for reorganizing politically bound and disorganized societies, trading directly with original resources owners, supporting intellectual liberalism and enlightened partnership instead of exploitative relationship.

What remains after your death is not your money, houses, cars, jets and possessions. All these can be destroyed by an army of enemies or your rebellious children and relatives in less than five years. Instead, what remains is the usefulness of your physical, emotional, industrial, artistic and intellectual contributions to the living's productive and responsible beliefs, institutions, discoveries, knowledge and socio-political structures. That is the guide and inspiration for human growth, the body of knowledge, motivation, beliefs and culture passed from generation to generation. That is the guarantee that meaningful life will persist after you are gone, and that the imperfection that scared you most in the world will not overcome humanity.

For writers, Albert Camus sums up our job description:
"The purpose of a writer is to keep civilization from destroying itself."

I believe in God as the creator of all things discovered and undiscovered. I cannot prove his existence to you, neither can you **prove** his non-existence to me. For all our means of verification are too limited to comprehend the mystery of our own being, before comprehending the mystery behind the essential EXISTENCE.

I believe because it is reasonable to believe that the power, order, beauty, motion and harmony in nature proceeds not from coincidence, but from an intelligent designer. And denying such EXISTENCE based on my imperfect means of sensual verification amounts to a logical fallacy of denying what I don't know, simply because I **cannot** understand it.

I believe that our deep feeling of responsibility for harmonizing growth in the world, what some people call conscience, is a deposit of that INTELLIGENT BEING in us. And we are free to choose to steadily respond or ignore its prompting for responsible productivity.

Finally, I believe that our demise from earth is but a continuation in the order of harmonizing growth in nature, and that in living by the natural principles of growth and harmony, death becomes a harmonious transition...

So, when I die, I don't want to be mourned, cried for or pitied!
I want to be celebrated and remembered when people gather to play, eat, drink, laugh, dance, love, give and work for common good. On that day, I want you to go out and be productive and socially responsible to your highest possible degree in line with the prompting of the intelligent and essential EXISTENCE. I love you…

Bibliography

BOOKS

1. Achebe, Chinua. *There was a country* (USA: Penguin books, 2012)
2. Aquinas, Thomas. *Summa Theologiae*
3. Aristotle, *Nicomachean ethics*
4. -----------, *Politics*, Bk I
5. Baker, Dean. *The conservative nanny state*, (Washington DC., Creative Commons, 2006).
6. Beauchamp, Tom and Childress, James. *Principles of biomedical ethics*, 5th edition (London: Oxford university press, 2001).
7. Chu, Appolus. *Time: our nemesis* (Port Harcourt: D Marcus & associates, 2016).
8. Coetzee and A. P. J. Roux (New York: Routledge, 2003).
9. Composta, Dario. *Moral philosophy and social ethics*, (Rome: Urbania University Press, 1987).
10. Cristiani, CH. L., *Un grand africain*, Lyon, Editions et Imprimérie du Sud-Est, 1956.APF, Scrit. Rif. Nei Congressi, Africa Angola, Vol. 9. 510-511.
11. Dowden, Richard. *Africa altered states, ordinary miracles.* (New York: Public Affairs, 2010).
12. Fadeiye, Oladele. *Essays on modern world history*, (Lagos: Murfat publications, 2009), p.190.
13. -------------------, *European conquest and African resistance* (Lagos: Murfat publications, 2011).
14. Hazlitt, Henry. *Economics in one lesson* (New York: Pocket books, Inc. 1946).
15. Hobbes, Thomas. *Leviathan,* edited by Michael Oakeshott (New York: Macmillan Publishing Company, 1962).
16. Kant, Immanuel. *Education,* translated by Annette Churton, (USA. University of Michigan press, 1966).
17. Kentenich, Joseph. *God's gentle rebel,* translated by Mary Cole and Christa Mucke (Mumbai: St. Paul's Press, 2008).
18. Machiavelli, *The Prince,* translated by C. E. Detmold (London: Wordsworth, 1997).
19. Mason, Alan. *Business bullseye: How to succeed in business,* (Canada: Broadview publishing, 2009).
20. Mondin, Battista. *Philosophical anthropology,* (Rome: Urbaniana University press, 1985).
21. Ogbimi, Francis E. *Solution to mass unemployment in Nigeria* (Ile-Ife: OAU Press, 2007).
22. Oladipo, Olusegun *The idea of African philosophy, 3rd edition* (Ibadab:

Hope publications, 2000).

23. Omoregbe, Joseph. *A simplified History of Western Philosophy,* (Joja press, Ikeja, Lagos, 1991).

24. ----------------------. *Ethics,* (Lagos: Joja press, 2004).

25. Peel, Michael. *A swamp full of dollars* (Ibadan: Bookcraft, 2010)

26. Plato, *Republic,* translated by John Llewelyn Davies and David James Vaughan (Wordsworth, 1997).

27. Ramose, Mogobe. "Discourses on Africa" in *The African Philosophy Reader, Second Edition,* Edited by P. H. Paul Glenn, *A tour of the Summa of St. Thomas Aquinas,* (USA: Tan Books and Publishers Inc., 1978)

28. Rodney, Walter. *How Europe underdeveloped Africa, 2009 edition,* (Abuja: Panaf press, 2009).

29. Tse, Edward. *The China strategy* (USA: Perseus Books, 2010)

30. Ufere, Anthony. *The good nurse* (Lagos: Sebana books, 2008)

31. Williams, Glanville. *Learning the law, 14th Edition* (Britain: Thomson Reuters, 2010).

32. Yew, Lee Kwan. *From third world to first* (USA: HarperCollins, 2000).

33. Universal declaration of human rights

34. V, *The mafia manager* (New York: St Martin's Griffin, 1997)

INTERNET MATERIALS

35. Ayn Rand, *The Nature of Government,* https://campus.aynrand.org/works/1963/12/01/the-nature-of-government/page2/

36. Brainy quotes, www.brainyquotes.com

37. Chukwunwike Enekwechi, "Africa's mixed economy: freedom without responsibility" in *Restartnaija,* 27th November, 2018. https://restartnaija.com/2018/11/27/africas-mixed-economy-irresponsible-freedom/

38. --------------, "Education in Nigeria, liberation or indoctrination?" in *Restartnaija.* 23rd November, 2017. https://restartnaija.com/2017/11/23/education-liberation-indoctrination/

39. --------------, "Fighting corruption in Nigeria with the wrong tool" in *Restartnaija,* 12th September, 2017. https://restartnaija.com/2017/09/12/fighting-corruption-in-nigeria-wrong-tool/

40. --------------, "Entrepreneurship on a leaking foundation, e dey patch am, e dey leak" in *Restartnaija,* 7th August, 2018. https://restartnaija.com/2018/08/07/entrepreneurship-e-dey-

patch-e-dey-leak/

41. --------------, "From Human to Patriot, more emotional than mechanical" in *Restartnaija,* 11th September, 2018. https://restartnaija.com/2018/09/11/human-patriot-emotional-mechanical/

42. --------------, "From social condemnation to social redemption: smartness vs greatness" in *Restartnaija,* 18th June, 2019. https://restartnaija.com/2019/06/18/from-society-condemnation-social-redemption/

43. --------------, "Fulfilling your mission in Nigeria before running away" in *Restartnaija,* 25th January 2018. https://restartnaija.com/2018/01/25/fulfilling-your-mission-in-nigeria/.

44. --------------, "installing the behavioural antivirus in kids before they leave the factory: family" in *Restartnaija,* 26th February, 2019. https://restartnaija.com/2019/02/26/installing-behavioural-antivirus-kids/.

45. --------------, "Is the truth always bitter?" in *Restartnaija,* 15th January, 2019. https://restartnaija.com/2019/01/15/the-truth-always-bitter/.

46. --------------, "Has the West become the demon of the world?" in *Restartnaija,* 3rd February, 2018. https://restartnaija.com/2018/02/03/has-the-west-become-demon-of-the-world/.

47. --------------, "Law as a tool of philosophy" in *Restartnaija,* 22nd February, 2018. https://restartnaija.com/2018/02/22/law-for-philosophy-legitimacy-and-common-good/.

48. --------------, "Leading a family beyond financial security to fulfilment" in *Restartnaija,* 7th May, 2019. https://restartnaija.com/2019/05/07/leading-family-beyond-finance/

49. --------------, "Let's make Nigeria great again… how great? We will get there… Where?" in Restartnaija 17th July, 2019. https://restartnaija.com/2019/07/17/lets-make-nigeria-great-again/0.

50. --------------, "Managing the danger of freedom in a modern and complex world" in *Restartnaija,* 6th November, 2018. https://restartnaija.com/2018/11/06/managing-freedom-complex-world/.

51. --------------, "Organizing the true national conference for a new Nigeria" in *Restartnaija,* 5th February, 2019. https://restartnaija.com/2019/02/05/organizing-nigerian-national-conference/.

52. --------------, "Our leaders for where, our brotherly jailers they are" in *Restartnaija,* 28th October, 2017. https://restartnaija.com/2017/10/28/our-leaders-our-brotherly-jailers/.

53. --------------, "Political parties and the distraction from development in Nigeria" in *Restartnaija,* 14th August 2018. https://restartnaija.com/2018/08/14/political-parties-distraction-development-nigeria/.

54. --------------, "Protecting Nigeria from foreign exchange manipulations" in *Restartnaija,* 10th December, 2018. *https://restartnaija.com/2018/12/10/protect-nigeria-exchange-rate/.*

55. --------------, "racism and the spirit of sportsmanship" in *Restartnaija,* 29th May, 2018. https://restartnaija.com/2018/05/29/racial-rivalry-sportsmanship/

56. --------------, "redirecting religious structures for productivity in Africa" in *Restartnaija,* 23rd April 2019. https://restartnaija.com/2019/04/23/redirect-religious-structures/.

57. --------------, "Repositioning Nigerian education for productivity and progress" in *Restartnaija,* 21st April, 2018. https://restartnaija.com/2018/04/21/repositioning-nigerian-education/

58. --------------, "The midwife leader: the leader Nigeria needs" in *Restartnaija,* 23rd March, 2018. https://restartnaija.com/2018/03/23/midwife-leader-leader-nigeria-needs/.

59. --------------, "The necessary pride for Nigeria's redemption" in *Restartnaija,* 27th August, 2019. https://restartnaija.com/2019/08/27/necessary-pride-nigeria-redemption.

60. --------------, "The politics of charity and baseless motivational speeches" in *Restartnaija,* 7th October, 2017. https://restartnaija.com/2017/10/07/politics-of-charity-and-motivation/.

61. --------------, "Transforming Nigeria's intertribal bitterness to neo-colonial liberation energy" in *Restartnaija,* 13th August, 2019. https://restartnaija.com/2019/08/13/transforming-nigeria-intertribal-bitterness/

62. --------------, "when 'living-to-have' overtakes having to live, we suffer" in *Restartnaija.* https://restartnaija.com/2019/02/12/when-living-to-have-overtakes-having-to-live-we-suffer/

63. --------------, "why give money to the church? Justification for church donations in the new era" in *Restartnaija,* 25th September,

2018. https://restartnaija.com/2018/09/25/why-give-church-justify-church-donations/.

64. Johann Wolfgang Von Goethe 1826, conferred from Antonio Frasconi, www.americanart.si.edu/artwork/there-is-nothing-more-frightful-than-ignorance-action-goethe-1826-series-great-ideas-western-man/

65. Joshua Akinwumi, "I nearly ran mad when my mother died few days after I travelled to England" in *Punch*, 21, July 2018. https://punchng.com/i-nearly-ran-mad-when-my-mother-died-few-days-after-i-travelled-to-england-akinwumi/

66. "Law: Meaning, Nature and Characteristics" in *Kullabs* https://www.kullabs.com/classes/subjects/units/lessons/notes/note-detail/6798

67. Mallence Bart-Williams, Change your channel, TED x Talks, 26th June 2015.

68. Martin Pengelly, "Georgetown students vote to pay reparations for slaves sold by university" in *The Guardian*, 15th April, 2019. www.theguardian.com/world/2019/apr/15/georgetown-students-reparations-vote-slaves-sold-by-university.

69. m.youtube.com/watch?v=AfnruW7yERA

70. Paul McDaniel, "What is international politics?" in *Classroom*, September 29, 2017. https://classroom.synonym.com/what-is-international-relations-12079692.html/.

71. Simon W. Blackburn, "Philosophy and logic" in *Britannica*. https://www.britannica.com/topic/truth-philosophy-and-logic.

72. http://www.yourdictionary.com/sincerity

73. Restartnaija, episode 15 https://youtu.be/osW1zihm12s

74. http://www.differencebetween.com/difference-between-civil-law-and-criminal-law/

75. St. Augustine, Quoted In the memorial analysis of Martin Luther King Junior, in *An Unjust Law Is No Law At All: Excerpts from "Letter from a Birmingham Jail"* https://home.isi.org/unjust-law-no-law-all-excerpts-letter-birmingham-jail, January 20, 2014.

76. United States Declaration of Independence, https://en.wikipedia.org/wiki/United_States_Declaration_of_Independence

MOVIES

77. *24 Season 1-9*, by Joel Surnow, et al.

78. 3:10 to Yuma, by James Mangold and Elmore Leonard, 2007.

79. *Game of Thrones*, Season 1-8, by David Benioff and D. B Weiss

80. *La Casa De Papel*, by Alex Pina, 2017-2018.
81. *No escape*, Mitchell Litvak, David Lancaster, Drew Dowdle, 2015.
82. *Spartacus*, by Steven S. Deknight et al. 2010. Season 1
83. *Married life*, directed by Ira Sachs, 2007.
84. *Lord of war*, Andrew Niccol, 2005.

* Note: The quotes attributed to Restartnaija are excerpts from Chukwunwike Enekwechi's talks, videos and articles.

DAILY SELF-CONTROL

Month: .... Year: ....

	1	2	3	4	5	6	7	8	9	10	11	12	13	14	15	16	17	18	19	20	21	22	23	24	25	26	27	28	29	30	31
P.E																															

Name: .... Witness: ....

Contact: .... Signature: .... Date: ....

Name: .... Witness: ....

Contact: .... Signature: .... Date: ....

For your privacy, cut off this DSC copy from the dotted line and keep for you and your witness alone.